Ed,

You know you are more than a friend. Everyone hopes or should hope they find @ least one(1) mentor or role model in their lives. ~~God~~ blessed me to be able to office next door to ~~someone~~ who was & is both to me for **12**years.

Merry Christmas to you & Betty & family.

Even if you have read this ~~book~~ you may agree it is worth @ least one(1) read a year!

Frank & Jason
& Debbie, Leslie
& Ashlyn

GOD SMILES *for* ME

Why Death Could Not Hold Me

To Judge Ed -
May God Smile
For You Too.

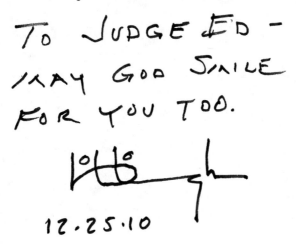

12.25.10

Why death could not hold me

GOD SMILES *for* ME

Raymond L. Burroughs

Ambassador International
GREENVILLE, SOUTH CAROLINA & BELFAST, NORTHERN IRELAND

www.ambassador-international.com

GOD SMILES FOR ME
Why death could not hold me

© 2009 Raymond L. Burroughs

Printed in the United States of America

Paperback ISBN:
978-1-935507-09-3

Hardback ISBN:
978-1-935507-16-1

Cover Design & Page Layout by David Siglin of A&E Media

AMBASSADOR INTERNATIONAL
Emerald House
427 Wade Hampton Blvd.
Greenville, SC 29609, USA

www.ambassador-international.com

AMBASSADOR PUBLICATIONS
Providence House
Ardenlee Street
Belfast, BT6 8QJ, Northern Ireland, UK
www.ambassador-productions.com

The colophon is a trademark of Ambassador

Dedication

This book is dedicated to my precious Pat, my wife, my friend, my soul mate, and the love of my life; to my children and all the other earthly angels who have contributed so much to help me find joy and success in this journey called life; and to the glory of God, who through Grace and healing has helped me find peace.

God Smiles for Me is a thoroughly enjoyable read, especially the poetry. A miraculous and engrossing tale, Raymond's story is a life-lesson that demonstrates what God can do when we live with faith. A powerful and inspirational story told well.

— Jane Ray, Educator

Wow, *God Smiles for Me* is a real page-turner, gripping the heart and mind so powerfully one cannot wait to read the next chapter. It is a story of hope, of physical and mental battles, where Raymond's faith in God and the healing power of Christ's love shine through like a beacon.

— Ralph Hendricks, Structural Engineer

God Smiles for Me is excellent, a real page-turner and a truly inspiring work! If only everyone could peer through the gloom and uncertainty and see the hand of God as Raymond Burroughs has done, my oh my, would the world be a better place. A great witness indeed!!

— Rev Dr. Peter Harrington, Minister

Raymond Burroughs' wonderful *God Smiles for Me* is both a moving testimonial and a fascinating, compelling story. He is a gifted writer, and his unique experiences – related here in clear, beautiful prose – is the stuff of a fine book indeed, and an important one.

— Ron Rozelle, author of *Into That Good Night* and *The Windows of Heaven.*

God Smiles for Me is inspirational. An in depth witness to one man's faith, it shares Raymond Burroughs' great life experience, leaving no doubt that only through the Grace of God did he survive to tell the story. Worthwhile reading, it offers a wonderful place to learn more about living a Christian life and the healing power of God.

— Ralph David, Bank Executive and Investor

A Note From The Author

In 1975, at the age of thirty-three, I was operated on for the removal of a massive tumor that was pressing on my brain stem. I was told I had less than six weeks to live. Soon after learning of the tumor I promised God I would tell the story to the world if I survived.

I've tried hard to live up to that promise. My most recent effort to tell the story is completion of GOD SMILES FOR ME. This book is much more than a memoir, it is a story not only of a man but of a multitude of miracles that began subtly at first but then, with ever growing momentum, literally redefined the purpose and direction of a very complex life.

All that I have, all I have done or accomplished, all I have experienced or enjoyed in this world since that miraculous survival, has clearly been a bonus, a gift of Healing Grace from the loving God who gave me a second chance at life.

It has been an amazing journey. Fortunately I haven't had to make it alone. Acknowledging and thanking all of the people who helped Pat and me reach this point in our lives without omitting someone would be impossible. For that reason, the only names not changed in this story are those of our immediate family.

So, I say to you one and all, our prayer warriors and angels on earth, thank you, thank you, thank you. You know who you are, and our loving God does too.

Make it a God filled life,
RAYMOND
October 9, 2008

Reading *God Smiles for Me* cover to cover in one evening, I was caught up in the sweet recounting of Raymond Burroughs' brush with eternity. Raymond carefully takes you through his experience with heartwarming and heart-stopping detail. Both his experiences and his miraculous recovery give testimony to the goodness of our God.

— Susan Moore, owner, Sonshine Book and Gift Shop

God Smiles for Me is absolutely marvelous. It is an inspirational, especially moving Christian message. Flowing without effort, Raymond Burroughs' writing is quite effective; the voice strong, the dialogue excellent, the description beautiful. This extraordinary true story kept me reading way into the night.

— Patricia Soledade, Freelance Editor

Driven by a promise to share his miracle with the world, author Raymond Burroughs lays his soul bare in an honest heartfelt rendering of his brush with mortality and his faith in God. It is a must read for all walks of life and most especially for those facing impossible odds. In *God Smiles for Me*, Burroughs delivers on his promise.

— Bill Cornwell, Editor & Publisher, *The Facts Newspaper*

Raymond Burroughs' story of faith and courage needed to be told. Challenged in my own faith, by his testimony, I was especially moved as I read of the initial reaction of his children following his devastating surgery. I found myself asking "If that were me what would I have done?" *God Smiles for Me* documents with clarity that God is good even when it seems that life is not.

— Ken Christoffersen, Pastor, Church of the Nazarene, Lake Jackson, TX

Table of Contents

Prologue

The breaking dawn tolls across the land
Heaven's promise for those who care
And yet we slumber, unaware
The day is close at hand
We yearn to love, but know not how
This time called life, this place called now.

I'm Raymond Burroughs. I'm an architect, a dreamer, and an eternal optimist. I'm also a Christian. I've seen the miracle of God's healing grace.

On October 9, 1975, I was operated on for the removal of an acoustic neuroma, a monstrous tumor at the base of my brain that was an immediate threat to my life. I was thirty-three years old, the same age Christ was when He was crucified.

Less than forty-eight hours before the operation, the neurosurgeon who was to be God's instrument in saving my life spent several agonizing hours trying to impress on my wife, Pat, and me the impact of the medical ordeal about to befall us. More than a few times during the conversation he paused to question whether we understood or not. He was concerned by the calm, almost matter-of-fact way we were accepting the death sentence he was predicting for me. Death or worse were the words he used.

He didn't know that the peace he saw on the outside merely reflected God's strength we felt on the inside. We were scared, and the fact that we might soon be separated by death made us feel sad. But we also knew that God was on our side, and regardless of what happened, we would sooner or later be together again.

Please don't misunderstand; the grace of acceptance of God's will did not come easily. For several months, since first learning of the tumor, we passed through all the normal phases that individuals facing death seem to experience. First came disbelief and defiance, then anger and frustration, followed by self-pity and the "why me?" syndrome, then mourning and grief at the idea of our own passing, and finally acceptance of the fact that the matter was no longer optional or in our hands.

During those weeks, in a vain attempt to crowd as much living as possible into my remaining days, we did everything for the last time. We went to the beach for the last time, watched each sunset as though it were the last, went fishing for the last time, made love for the last time (many times), and did all the other earthly things that suddenly become so precious when you realize you are about to lose them.

We also began to find strength in prayer, and the Christian training of our youth began to pay dividends. Our family drew closer, became more aware of each other as individuals and of the beauty and value of all that was around us.

This is the story, not of a man, but of a multitude of miracles that began subtly at first but then, with ever growing momentum, literally redefined the purpose and direction of a very complex life. It is my personal experience with hope and promise, the power of prayer and the healing grace of God.

The First Miracle
Summer 1975 / Texas Gulf Coast

Waves capped white
Breakers roar
Sea shelled sand
Tide washed shore
Windblown green
Dunes piled high
Shorebirds preen
Seagulls sigh
And time looks back at me.

Thank God we discovered the tumor in time to do something before it was too late. During a routine hearing test, a local doctor noticed I was also having balance problems. He ordered further tests in Galveston. The diagnosis: acoustic neuroma! The prognosis: critical nerve damage portending imminent death.

The doctor, a recently introduced friend and the only ear, nose and throat specialist in our area, had his office in a historically restored house in Freeport, Texas, a small town on the Gulf Coast just six miles south of the community of Lake Jackson where we lived. I had gone to see him on the afternoon of the day I discovered my left ear had quit working. An hour earlier, the voice on the other end of my business call had gone silent in the middle of a sentence. Moving the telephone to the other ear made it clear the problem wasn't with the telephone connection. Something was wrong in my head.

The waiting room was claustrophobic. I could smell the musty swirl of dust particles drifting lazily about in the warm sun rays coming through the cut-glass transom above the heavily antiqued entry doors. Much to close for comfort, an older couple waited patiently, both coughing coarsely now and then as they leaned together to share an article in a dog eared National Geographic Magazine.

Soon after they were called back, I too was in one of the old bedrooms that served as a combination lab and examining room. A few minutes after beginning my examination the doctor diagnosed me as having acute hearing loss due to bruising from percussion impact. He attributed it to my passion for wing shooting. Blasts from the thousands of rounds of shotgun shells I fired each year at my hunting lease in Mexico must have gradually damaged the nerve.

His explanation didn't make sense. I fired the shotgun from my right shoulder, meaning the shells and the blasts exhausted on the right side. "Why the left ear?" I asked, more concerned than ever.

"It's probably only temporary," he reassured me. "Sometimes an acoustic nerve will heal itself; if the initial damage isn't too severe and additional abuse is avoided."

He proposed making a set of custom molded earplugs that would protect my ears from further damage. "How long will that take?" I asked, "The Mexican dove hunting season opens in a couple of months."

He just smiled and shook his head. Even though I had only known him for a few months, he already knew making light of a serious situation was my way of buying time to sort things out.

A few weeks later his office called. The earplugs were ready. I headed toward the coast to pick them up, thinking I might swing by my favorite beach on the way back. Beautiful and remote, especially in the dry summer months when the bordering Brazos River was running clear at its mouth where it emptied into the Gulf, Bryan Beach was a timeless, unchanging place I often visited when I needed to put things into perspective. That long and lonely stretch of sand, the solitude, the unfathomable distance to the horizon, the lure of what lay beyond, the mystery beneath the unseen depths, and the constancy of the wind and waves, their sounds and smells, all seem to speak to me, calming my soul and strengthening my belief in God's universal order of things.

The doctor was pleased to see me. The earplugs fit perfectly. With them on I could hear normal conversation through my right ear, but louder noises were filtered out. "The left plug seems redundant," I told him. "I still can't hear a thing on that side."

He just shook his head and changed the subject.

For once, he seemed to have time on his hands. We chatted about hunting for a few minutes, and then I turned to leave. As I often did, being large, an ex-jock, I bumped the door frame on the way out. The doctor followed, watching closely, as I headed down the hall to the waiting room.

When I reached the front desk, he looked at me, visibly concerned. "Were you aware you bumped the door frame back there?"

"Happens all the time," I laughed, "especially in an old building like this. In the early days they didn't make doors big enough for guys like me."

His expression didn't change. "I think we'd better do some more tests.

By the end of the next week my wife Pat and I were at the University of Texas Medical Branch in Galveston seeing a doctor that specialized in inner ear problems. Standing on one foot, then the other, walking a chalk line, and enduring the rush of cold water being sprayed in my ears while describing the weird, oscillating light patterns being projected on the wall, I almost passed out. Soon I was dizzy, the room spinning, the colors morphing into one. It became increasingly difficult to maintain my balance. Hopelessly drunk, I tasted hot bile rising in my throat. My senses over stimulated, I almost threw up.

When the testing was over, we were told to wait in the sparse lobby, a stuffy, clinical, institutional space of blues and greens and grays with overstuffed furniture and no windows. No wonder it took a half hour to regain my composure. Finally the nurse who had done the testing came out. A large Hispanic woman with a positive air of good cheer, she had an inscrutable smile on her face.

"Well, what did you find out?"

Her expression didn't change. "Nothing definite yet. We'll send the results to the doctor for his analysis. I'm sure he'll be calling you before long. Don't worry; he's one of the best in his field. I'm sure everything will work out just fine."

Luckily Pat was along to drive us home. Badly disoriented, I would have probably driven us into the bay on one side of the road or the Gulf on the other. Or perhaps, been stopped by a Galveston patrolman and asked to walk another line; a sobriety test I most certainly would have failed miserably.

The sunlight and surf, normally a panorama of spectacular sights along the Blue Water Highway linking Galveston and Brazoria County, went almost unnoticed as we turned our thoughts inward on the seemingly longer than normal drive home. Something was in the air. Something foul: something more foul than the stench of rotting seaweed that covered the short stretch of narrow beach bordering the highway soon after we crossed the toll bridge at San Luis pass.

As we approached the even taller bridge that spans the Inter-coastal Canal near the small resort community of Surfside, where the highway turns north toward Lake Jackson, it finally occurred to me what the nurse had said that was so upsetting. At the crest of the bridge, almost to heaven it seemed, I startled Pat with an unanswerable question, the first of many highly emotional outbreaks that would haunt us for months to come.

"Don't worry! Don't worry about what?" I yelled.

Pat was putting on a brave front, but it was obvious she was concerned too. Her usual reassuring smile was slow to come. But come it did. And her words were what I needed for the moment. "It's okay, honey." she said quietly. "Whatever comes we'll handle together. And God will help us."

Not knowing was bad. But the waiting to find out was worse. Almost a month passed before my local doctor's nurse called. He wanted to see me right away. I was there within the hour. The waiting room was more crowded than on the previous visit but they ushered me right into his office. A few minutes later he was behind his overloaded desk, trying to look casual but fooling no one but himself.

He opened a file and studied it for a minute. "Raymond," he said, his voice softer than usual, "I'm afraid we've got a worse problem than we thought."

"It's okay," I said. "I can live with one ear. The hearing's perfect in the right one. I'll just have to remember to wear the earplugs." I had already had time to steel myself for the news I was permanently deaf in my left ear.

"It's worse than that." He picked up a weathered book from his cluttered credenza, walked around the desk and sat in a wingback chair across from me. Opening the book to a marked page, he studied it a moment then looked directly into my eyes. When he finally spoke his voice was almost a whisper. "You have an acoustic neuroma."

"A what?" Now I was really getting nervous.

"A tumor on your acoustic nerve."

Tumors meant cancer. Cancer meant death. My stomach knotted. Seeing I was rattled, he moved to a chair beside me, put his hand on my shoulder, and gave me time to compose myself. I hardly heard him continue. "It's probably not malignant, but it has to be pretty advanced to have pinched off your eighth nerve that suddenly. The problem is if it's not removed it may pinch off other more critical nerves at any time."

"Wait a minute Doc, you're going too fast," I almost shouted. "What do you mean, pinch off other nerves? You said it wasn't malignant. Can't you fix this thing?"

"I can't. It would take a neurosurgeon, a really good neuro-surgeon, using state of the art equipment." He said, handing me the open medical book, pointing to a paragraph as he read.

My mind was reeling. My eyes blurred as I stared at the page.

ACOUSTIC NEUROMA: Benign tumor…eighth nerve…com-pressed cranial ventricle…loss of hearing then loss of…heart, breath-ing…eventual death due to primary functional failure. Probability of abatement at advanced stages rare.

My voice sounded like it was coming from the bottom of a well. "Are you telling me I'm going to die? And you can't do anything about it? What kind of a doctor are you? What kind of a friend are you? What am I supposed to do?"

Hearing the outbreak, the nurse came into the office and closed the door behind her. "Maybe we'd better call your wife," the doctor suggested, nodding to the nurse.

I turned to the nurse. "No. Wait. I need some time to think this through." Before they could respond I was racing down the hall. I could hear the doctor following closely behind me.

"I'm sorry Raymond. Procedures for microsurgery of this type are still in the experimental…"

I was out of the door and in my car, throwing it into reverse and flooring the accelerator. I skidded out of the small parking lot, almost running over the teenage couple crossing the drive. It was like a bad dream. I was in a state of disbelief.

Soon I turned to outright denial. There was no way that doctor could be right. I was thirty-three years old, in the prime of my life. I was young, strong, and bulletproof. I had a beautiful wife, two wonderful kids and a sick mother-in-law who depended on me. I had a promising career. There were things I wanted to do. Things I needed to do. My life had hardly begun. There was a lot of living left to be done.

Somehow I ended up at the beach. Rolling down the car windows, I stopped on the sand. My favorite refuge seemed alien and gray. The sky was overcast, misty, darkened to the point the horizon of sky and sea became one. The water was muddied, the waves heavy with foam. The beach, littered with seaweed and trash, was devoid of life. No shorebirds, no seagulls, not even a scrambling sand crab. It smelled of death. The humid gulf breeze, suffocating as it saturated the car, bore the taste of stale salt.

By then I was mad. It wasn't fair. I had done nothing wrong. Why was God letting this happen to me? I scrambled out of the car and headed for the sea. Forgetting my new pin-striped suit, fancy patterned leather shoes and red power tie, the uniform of choice for a young and aspiring company vice-president, I walked right into that pulsating surf. Hot and grasping, the swallowing swells were soon at my waist. Gritty sand eroded beneath me. The unseen undertow pulled at my pants legs. Raising a shaking fist into the air, I shouted to the heavens. "God, I'm going to beat this thing!" Then, the wind out of me, I almost went down. My life was over, my dreams destroyed, my hope vanquished. My destiny was no longer my own. This time the challenge was bigger than me.

Head down, defeated, I returned to the car. Slamming the door, I turned the key and stomped on the accelerator. The car didn't move. Stuck! I was stuck in the sand. With life running out, suspended in time, in a place all alone by the sea. Folding my arms over the steering wheel, I put my head down and cried.

How long I wept there, I do not know, but by the time I looked up the world had changed. Rays of the setting sun filtered through breaking clouds, now a crimson red. The white capped waves were dancing dunes of gold. Sliding remnants of the surging surf caressed the silvered sand, a silent serenade to the passing day. Search-

ing seagulls drifted near and far. Shorebirds skittered in and out of
the water along endless tide-swept shore. Never had I seen a more
beautiful end to the day. Perhaps, I thought, God had heard my
plea. No longer angry, just drained, I got out of the car and walked
back out into the surf.

Tears and sea mist mingled as one as I lifted up my open palm
to the glorious heavens above. "God," I said prayerfully, "If it's your
will, we're going to beat this thing." As I watched in awe, the clouds
parted and the magnificent orange ball of the sun slowly settled below the glowing horizon. No longer afraid, I waded back toward the
beach. Reaching the shoreline, I turned about once more, shouting
toward the darkening sea and sky. "And when we do," I promised,
"I'll tell the world."

The moment those words left my lips something changed. I no
longer felt afraid. I no longer felt alone. And I knew, I knew in my heart
and soul, that with God's help whatever was to come we would handle
together. My salvation was no longer up to me. God was in charge and
God's will would be done. And I would live to tell the story.

Even with that revelation, for a very brief moment I hesitated,
wondering how I could be so sure that God really heard. God's
answer came instantly and the proof wasn't far behind. The heavens
didn't open up, and thunder didn't roar, but a gentle peace envel-
oped me. The pounding of the surf became one with the rhythm
of my heart. The evening breeze, chilling my wet body only moments before, became a warm caress that urged me on my way.

Returning to the car, forgetting about being hopelessly
stuck, I started the engine and drove off that lonely beach toward the waiting arms of my family. As I felt the tires grip the
solid surface of the paved asphalt road, miraculously free from
the sand trap of moments before, it dawned on me what had
just happened. God had set me free.

His plan for me was already in action. The miracles were underway.

Questions

Red Cardinal crowned
Heart warming sight
Flame burnished bright
Spring's memories
Sing songs to me.

On automatic pilot, I headed home. A thousand questions bombarded my mind. What if God had another plan? What if I did die? How would Pat survive, all alone, struggling to support two children and an ailing mother? How would she explain to Ramona and Rob why their daddy had gone away? Not for a weekend hunt, but forever. How would I stand being separated from them? Would my precious children even remember me?

It saddened me to think how much I would be letting them down. Our daughter Ramona, at eight, might remember a little. But Robert, our three year old son, probably wouldn't remember a thing about me.

On the other hand, I knew from personal experience, children understand and retain more than we think sometimes. Or maybe God just speaks to them in a special voice. Ramona had demonstrated that clearly when she was three years old.

Tears blurred my eyes as my mind drifted back to that very special day soon after Ramona's third birthday. About a year before, following a very short illness, Pat's father, Ernest O'Neil, had died of cancer. One day he was there, bouncing his only grandchild on his knee, and then, in what seemed a blink of the eye, he was gone. How truly innocent our daughter had been. And, as we were later to find out, wise too.

It was a day for remembering. The morning began with mockingbirds playing dodge among the sun-flecked shadows spreading across the lawn. Overhead a canopy of trees created an ever-changing pattern of light and green and gold as the autumn breeze fanned their leaves against the pale blue sky. The frost of the week before, a rare occurrence that early in the fall in north Louisiana, was already forgiven and forgotten. Old south warmth postponed the coming of winter for another day. Pat and I relaxed on the patio soaking up the soothing sun while Ramona plucked sweet smelling purple blossoms from the winter clover that had at last gained a hold in the browning Bermuda grass. We talked softly, reliving the sadness of the previous year. Our conversation was light but our hearts were heavy. We were thinking of Ernest O'Neil.

Ernest, as proud of his Irish heritage as his American birth, was a large man with a rectangular face, bold forehead, boxcar ears and a smile that could brighten the darkest day. His laugh, spontaneous and frequent, brought joy to those who knew him. And many did know him, for his job as an executive for the Kansas City Southern Railroad Company took him on frequent jaunts stretching from Kansas City to New Orleans, a path that brought him in contact with public officials, railroad employees, travelers, and working men and women at every level of society. Never forgetting a name or a face, he treated all he met with equal respect. People just naturally liked Ernest O'Neil. And if they were honest, hardworking, and fair, he liked them too.

Pat, his only child, was the love of his life. Our daughter Ramona was the joy his life. We all looked forward to his frequent visits. Ernest was a stabilizing factor in our lives. Someone we could always count on to care and help, and someone who would always be there when we needed guidance or encouragement. Or so we hoped and thought. But it wasn't meant to be.

On a beautiful, late fall day, following an abundance of hugs and kisses from his only grandchild, we took Ernest to the hospital for what he said was to be a routine checkup. He never went home again. Less than a month later, he was dead of cancer. The following Sunday we buried him as a cold drizzling rain drenched the still warm earth and the last of summer followed him to his grave. That evening we finally faced the painful task of telling Ramona that her granddaddy would not be coming again.

Pat, as usual with our first born, took the lead.

"Yes Mommy," Ramona nodded, "Granddaddy has gone to Heaven to be with God. But Granddaddy will come to supper again."

"No Honey, he can't come. He'll be in Heaven for a long, long time."

"Then someday we'll go to Heaven to see him."

"Yes dear, someday we will."

With that she seemed content. She accepted her mother's words with a childlike faith, hugged us both noticeably longer than usual and quietly went to sleep.

After that, she seldom spoke of Ernest, and when she did it was with a detachment that suggested a memory rapidly vanishing. We were saddened by the possibility that she might forget him, but grateful she was spared the pain and loneliness we were experiencing. Now a full year had passed since his death and it had been many months since she had mentioned him at all.

The chattering of the mockingbirds was suddenly interrupted as she came running toward us, calling in an excited voice.

"Daddy! Mommy! Come see the little bird."

Trembling with excitement, she took our hands in hers and led us to the back of the yard. On the sandy red river soil laid a colorful Cardinal. At first it appeared he was taking a dust bath beneath the holly hedge. But nearby a tuft of pink down swaying slowly in the breeze told another story.

"See Daddy, the little bird can't fly." Then in an optimistic tone, "But he'll be all right in a little while."

I hesitated, and then told the truth. "No, Darling, the little bird is dead."

"Well, he can rest a while, and then he can fly high up in the sky with the other birds."

"No Honey, the little bird is dead. He's gone to heaven to be with God."

"Why is the little bird dead, Daddy?"

The "eternal why". How could I answer? At three years old our daughter couldn't possibly understand the meaning of death for she had yet to grasp the concept of life. I turned to her mother for support. Pat's tearful eyes and trembling lip made it clear she was still thinking of her father. It was up to me to make our daughter understand this time.

Turning to Ramona, her trusting face now focusing on me, I realized there was only one way any of us can accept what we can't comprehend.

FAITH! The answer was faith. The same faith that made it possible for us to endure our loss could answer a child's "why" about life or death or anything else. Faith doesn't depend on age, experience, education or understanding. It only requires acceptance of, and trusting in, a loving God.

"Sugar," I said, trying to speak in a way she could understand, "This little bird probably had a happy life singing pretty songs and flying about up in the sky. One time he was a baby bird and lived with his mother and daddy. Then he grew up and had little baby birds of his own. Finally he grew old and tired. So he died. He closed his eyes and went to sleep forever. Now he's in Heaven with God and he won't ever be tired again. Sooner or later, everyone, every living creature, dies and goes home to be with God. That's the way God planned it."

"Will the little bird sing pretty songs in heaven?"

"I'm sure he will, honey."

I picked up the bird and carefully placed it on a deep pile of autumn colored leaves. As it sank out of sight I thought sure another "Why?" would follow. But the question didn't come. Ramona, satisfied for the moment at least, headed for the gym set. Soon the swing was stretching to its limits, her sun brightened hair flowing freely out behind while small sandaled feet strained without success to touch the cloud studded sky

The day ended as beautifully as it began. Weary from a day in the fresh air, our little daughter climbed into her bed without the usual procrastination and hugged us both good night. Just as we turned to leave she called out in her smallest little girl voice.

"Daddy?"

"Yes, honey?"

"Will the little bird sing to Granddaddy?"

Pat turned a sad but joyous smile in my direction. There was a different kind of tears in her eyes this time. The expression of grief and pain that had been evident throughout the day was replaced by a look of grace and acceptance.

"Yes, darling," I answered, "I'm sure he will."

For the first time in many months we were reassured that our precious daughter understood her granddaddy had died and was now in heaven with God. And equally important, we realized that her granddaddy was still alive in her memory and would live there, hopefully, for a long, long time…

The blare of a horn brought me back to the present. I braked sharply as a battered pickup truck full of teenagers whizzed by, missing a collision by only a few feet. I had turned off the highway onto a secondary street leading toward our neighborhood without looking. Their shouts of scorn were well deserved.

The near miss seemed to be a message. I wasn't dead yet, so maybe I shouldn't rush things. If a child could have faith, I could too. "God helps those who help themselves," my grandfather, Papa, had often said when I visited his farm as a child. For the moment, at least, I quit mourning the possibility of my own passing, bolstered my courage, and focused on getting safely home.

Home, Hope, and Helplessness

Grief, so like a winter fog
Comes in lifts and waves
A blanket on our earthbound souls
A veil both night and day
With vision dim we turn to Him
And pray
The pain my Lord is much too great
Please take this cloud away.

Within ten minutes I was pulling onto the driveway. Greeted by both kids at the door, it was all I could do to keep my composure. Paying no attention to the damp, seaweed smell of my filthy clothes, they showered me with kisses. By the time I turned to hug Pat, hot tears were running down my cheeks. She knew without asking something was terribly wrong.

I shook my head knowingly and whispered in her ear, "Later."

Coming out of the kitchen, wiping her hands with a dish towel, my mother-in-law, Ines, realized something was going on. Her coming to live with us was already proving to be a blessing. Recognizing our need for privacy she ushered the kids off to watch TV.

It took a while, but I finally was able to make Pat understand what the doctor had said. She showed no fear, only warmth, and love, and compassion. And unlike me, some degree of reason. In spite of my experience at the beach, I found it hard to offer much hope.

"But there must be something we can do," she said.

My head seemed to be splitting in two. I wondered if it was the tumor. "Six weeks. Six to eight weeks he said! The gift of prophecy or something? Reading from that medical book like St. Peter at the gate. Acoustic neuroma, he said. Benign tumor at the base of the brain. Pinching off the blood flow at the orifice where the primary nerves pass through the skull from the body into the brain. First the acoustic nerve, then the vision, the facial nerve, lungs, the heart, the…"

I didn't realize I was shouting.

"Oh, what the heck! Then you die. He read it out of a darn book! What kind of a doctor reads a book to tell a patient he is going to die? He didn't even know what an acoustic neuroma was until he read…"

Becoming alarmed, Pat glanced frightfully toward the living room where the kids were still watching *Mayberry RFD* on TV. She put her hands on my cheeks and tried to calm me down.

"Honey, please, you'll frighten the kids. Please, for me. Sit down and let's think this thing through."

Collapsing into a chair, I scrambled unsuccessfully to catch the glass of water I knocked over. Taking my trembling hands in hers, Pat kissed me on the forehead.

"Tell me exactly what the doctor said. After he read the book," she said softly.

I looked up, not at her, but through her, she later told me. She'd seen the look a thousand times when I was thinking about the design of one of my architectural or development projects. My mind was already miles away, searching for a creative answer. I answered her softly, as though talking to myself.

"He said there was nothing he could do. It would take a specialist. With state of the art tools. Then, as I was leaving, he shouted something about it being experimental."

"Howard!" she said, her hope obvious.

"What?"

"Howard. We'll call Howard. He'll know what to do. Howard always knows what to do. He's the best radiologist in Houston."

"Maybe he knows an undertaker," I quipped.

Pat started to cry. Now it was my turn to settle her down.

"Okay. Okay. It's worth a try. But it's a lot to dump on anyone, much less a friend like Howard."

"Let's call him now," she said, reaching for the phone.

Putting my hand over hers, I stopped her. She looked at me pleadingly.

"It's late," I told her. "Probably the longest day of my life. Maybe the last. Let's feed the kids then turn in early." I looked deeply into her eyes.

Understanding at once, she stepped close and hugged me tightly. "You sure you're up to it?"

I smiled weakly and kissed her.

"I'd bet my life on it. Without you there wouldn't be any sense living anyway."

Now there were tears in her eyes. "Oh, honey. That's all I've been able to think about since you told me about the tumor." She broke down and cried.

Looking over Pat's shoulder I could see the kids standing in the doorway, a questioning look on their faces. Ramona, eyes wide, came running toward us, her little brother Robert following close behind. Pat and I knelt down welcoming them into our embrace. They hugged us tightly and showered us with kisses totally unaware that life as they knew it was about to be turned upside down. How in the world, I wondered, were we ever going to make them understand?

Early the next morning we were on our way to Houston. Dr. Howard Lowe, a radiologist at the Houston Medical Center is a lifelong friend from our hometown of Shreveport, Louisiana. He could help us evaluate the alternatives. He was concerned but pleased we had called on him for help and advice. He told us a newly invented machine; a computer-controlled X-ray called a CATSCAN had just been installed at Methodist Hospital. It could map the brain and within minutes reveal the location and extent of the tumor.

We made the drive to the Houston Medical Center in record time. Located less than a block from Rice University where I did my graduate studies in Urban Design, near the Museum District, and just across the street from Hermann Park and the Zoo, it was in our favorite part of town. We had passed that way many times, and I had even spent a semester doing a design project planning for projected growth of the already massive medical complex. But being young and healthy, we had given little thought to the importance of what took place there or the life and death struggles that went on around the clock.

Now that we had a critical need, we saw the Medical Center from a new perspective. It seemed much larger and more complex; almost ominous.

Parking on an upper level of a huge, multi-storied garage, we were soon on the floor where Dr. Howard had his office. It was like a homecoming for Pat and her best childhood friend, but far too serious an occasion for us to forget for even a moment why we were there.

Dr. Howard personally escorted us to the imaging suite, a newly remodeled space, institutional but warm, thanks to the mauves and pinks of the walls and carpet and carefully choreographed illumination from recessed lighting. Strategically positioned spotlights accented the stainless steel tube encapsulating the state of the art imaging equipment that offered us hope and understanding of what we were up against.

After a brief tour and an explanation of what was going to take place, I lay back on the narrow table that extended into the tube and the nurse put a small pillow under my head. She seemed nervous. I was too. The table, though padded, was hard and cold; the tube I would slide headfirst into appeared much too small in diameter. Though softer than my college football days of a decade before, I was still a large man. It was going to be a tight fit.

I wanted to scream. When it came to courage, claustrophobia was my Achilles heel. Little did I know, it was one of the easiest medical procedures I would experience for a long time.

I could hear Howard talking to Pat behind the lead shield panel in the corner of the room. "It's called a CATSCAN. Just became available. Totally new technology, a miracle machine. It can show us clearly what we're up against."

An ominous buzz was the nurse's signal to clear the room. Pat rushed to my side taking my hands in hers, hanging on as long as she could as I slowly slid toward that ominous orifice. Our eyes locked in that silent communication only soul mates can share. Nothing needed to be said. The message was clear. Whatever was to come, we were in it together.

Howard put his arm around Pat, gave me a reassuring look, and led her to the door that led to the waiting room. "Don't worry little sister." He promised, "We'll get you two love birds through this."

Pat was an only child. Howard was as close to a brother as Pat would ever have. When she said he always knew the right thing to do, she truly believed it. I wasn't sure there was anything anyone could do.

I gritted my teeth as the tube engulfed me, my shoulders and elbows dragging on the smooth sides. There was a light inside and soft music playing. A lot like a casket with all the accessories, I thought. It smelled like a mixture of ether and rubbing alcohol. And nervous sweat.

A voice over the internal speaker told me not to move. Fat chance, I was wedged tight. The light dimmed and the music came back on. A mechanical hum began and my small eternity in purgatory began. I could taste the bile in my throat,

Just when I thought I could stand it no more, the light brightened, the music stopped, and I was slowly ejected. The first thing I heard was Howard's voice. As the nurse helped me sit up, I could see he was speaking to the young intern we had met in his office before we came into the x-ray suite. I stood and asked the nurse where I could find a restroom. She opened a back door and pointed down the hall, closing the door behind me as I hurried through.

Turning back to thank her, I noticed the muffled conversation coming through the door from the imaging suite had paused. Thinking Pat had joined the others, and wanting to hear what Howard had to say, I turned back. Cracking the door, I could hear Howard and his intern talking. Howard's voice sounded alarmed. I froze, straining to hear.

"Now look at this area, John." There was a long silence. "See that dark mass? About the size of my thumb. That's the tumor. It's huge. And it's pressing on his brain stem."

"What does it mean?" the younger man asked.

"It means Raymond's ENT was right." Focused on the bright monitor behind the screen, they were totally unaware I could hear them. "If something's not done soon there's a good chance Raymond is going to die. Maybe tonight, maybe in a few weeks. But one way or another, unless there is a miracle, it's going to happen."

I watched unseen as Howard walked over and opened the door to the hall where Pat was waiting just outside.

"What? What did you see?" Pat asked, hoping for some reassurance that everything would be all right.

"Raymond clearly has an Acoustic Neuroma, but until we have a chance to fully examine the data it's too soon to say for sure what we're up against," he told her with reservation.

I could hear Pat gasp. She must have thought he knew more than he was saying.

Before she could ask more he continued. "It's been a long day. You and Raymond go on home and try to get some rest. I'll call you in the morning after I've talked to a neurologist."

I coughed before I joined them in the hall. They fell silent when they saw me. No one knew I had heard a thing. But I had heard enough. The prognosis was clear. The massive tumor was threatening my brain stem. Only a short time to live. Maybe days; maybe weeks. Inoperable with conventional techniques.

"Doesn't sound to good," I commented, trying to put on a brave front as we got into the car.

Pat met my gaze, then quickly looked away, pretending not to see the tears forming at the corner of my eyes. Or perhaps to keep me from seeing hers. "No it doesn't," she said in a soft voice that was less than convincing. "But maybe it will when Howard calls tomorrow."

We drove home in silence. What more was there to say?

Unfamiliar Territory

Within young lives a story's told
Of hope, of love so strong and bold
So young, so new, so very pure
So wise, so right, yet immature.

Not surprisingly, the fifty mile drive home passed quickly. Both Pat and I spent most of the trip lost in our own thoughts. About the time we were clear of the crowded chaos on Houston's Inner Loop 610, and on the rural highway that headed toward the coast and home, reality set in.

I was in big trouble. Denial was no longer an option. Indifference was no longer an option. It seemed my guardian angel had abandoned me and I was no longer bulletproof. It was unfamiliar territory.

How could it be, I kept asking myself, that it might soon be over? How could I have a tumor without knowing it? Why me? Why now? It didn't make sense. I was a young man. I still had things to do. As far as I knew my life was neither a blessing nor a burden, to me, or to anyone else. So why was I being singled out to die?

As we got closer to home, my mind drifted back, reviewing the past and searching for clues. Other questions had been asked. Innocent enough at the time, they now seemed obvious premonitions that had gone unheeded.

Growing up was relatively easy. At home, my older brother, James, took the heat. He was the first born. Someone wanted. Someone wanted perfect. A good role model, but a hard act to follow. But me? I'm almost sure I was an accident. Just another mouth to feed. A product of escapism in a war torn world. As far as parenting went, I was pretty much on my own in those earlier years.

That wasn't all bad. It made me self-reliant. As a second son I had to try harder, run faster to get out of trouble, and talk and smile my way out of a lot of situations no one bothered to warn me about. Once I got the hang of it though, I was on my way. My father was rich and my mother good looking. And to hear me tell it, I wasn't so bad myself.

In the third grade the eighty-five-pound-league football coach learned I was tough. My father liked that. The girls at school liked my smile. My mother liked that. Suddenly the family noticed I was there. Not all there, they probably thought. But there.

During my childhood I had all the trappings of a good Christian life. As the second of four children, not much was expected of me. Most of time I was on my own, allowed to do as I pleased as long as I behaved. My father, a man of strong principles and unquestionable character, was a very successful businessman. My mother, a sensitive, loving and very sentimental woman, was a very good mother and housewife. Mama, my maternal grandmother, lived with us most of the time. She was a peaceful and loving woman who lived to be a hundred years old.

And then there was Papa; my paternal grandfather. A dirt farmer and a Methodist preacher in rural Arkansas, he was a great man in a small world. By the time I knew him, he was frail, bent, and old as Methuselah and his barn was about to fall down. Much of my childhood summers were spent visiting his tired, hard-rock farm in the foothills of the Ozarks.

His house was a quaint place with a steep roof and a porch on two sides. The stones on the exterior walls had been gathered by my father and his brothers from the creek bottom fields below the hill where the house precariously perched. The stucco was gray and the truncated columns on the porch were white. On the side by the drive and the gravel road that separated it from the barn and a makeshift garage with a Model-T inside, which you could see if you peeked through the cracks in the weathered board siding, was a hand dug well surrounded by a stone wall and covered by warped planks. It was an exciting moment for me, my older brother and our country cousins, when Papa opened the well, lowered the wooden bucket by its worn rope, and let us help pull it up heavy laden with iron flavored water sloshing to the top. We all got a taste from the same tin dipper, and we all made a face and spit it out, much to the delight of Papa. And us. It was one of the few things that would make him laugh.

Though usually serious, Papa always treated me like I was something special. Through his teachings and example, I learned about peace, the beauty of nature, and the hand of God in all things.

As a child I had a freckled face and big ears. And I thought I was ugly. Most of my country cousins appeared to think so too. As a "city slicker" I was an easy target for their teasing.

One day, while we played in Papa's rock fenced yard; the taunting got pretty rough. Someone said I looked like a polka-dotted taxicab coming down the street with the doors open. Another chimed in, saying no, more like a spotted elephant with his ears flapping. Soon they were all following me around, hands extending their ears or arms swinging from side to side like a trunk, their version of an elephant walk.

Finally, tears in my eyes, I couldn't take it anymore. I retreated to the side porch where I found Papa sitting in the swing. Before I could backtrack, he waved for me to join him. Papa was so old most of the kids were a little bit afraid of him. His bushy gray hair, thick eyebrows, penetrating eyes, deep voice, bent back and smell of an aging farmer were intimidating. But, since he was always nice to me, I wasn't afraid of him. He looked like an image of God I had seen in a Sunday school book.

He noticed I was unusually quiet. "What's the problem, boy? Why aren't you playing with the others?"

"Oh, it's nothing Papa, I'm just tired."

"Seems to me you're a little sad too," he said putting his arm around my shoulder and drawing me closer on the swing. Nobody fooled Papa. "Now tell me what this is all about."

I got teary again. "They make fun of me. They say I have ears as big as an elephant. And I do."

Papa was quiet for a long moment then he wiped a salty tear from my cheek and leaned forward to look me directly in the eye. "Tell me Raymond, who do you think gave you those ears?"

I thought a moment before the answer occurred to me. Papa was a preacher. The answer was obvious, even to a self-conscious, sweat covered kid. "God, I guess."

"You guess? Of course it was God who gave you those ears. God is good. And everything God does is good. So if those ears are good enough for God, don't you think they ought to be good enough for you?"

I sat silent but the message sank home.

He tousled my hair and laughed. "And they make you hear better too. Now get out there and show the others you can hold your own." From then on, I wore my big ears like a badge of honor.

Not all of Papa's lessons were so serious, but they all left me with an insight that would serve me well later in life. He truly believed you couldn't learn from experiences you weren't having. Most of the time these experiences with Papa were a lot of fun, but he was very old, and sometimes he got us both in some pretty impossible situations.

When I was eight years old, Papa decided it was time for me to learn how to milk a cow. Cows were scary. And they stunk. And the hay in the old barn made you itch. I said no, but he insisted. Herded into the dilapidated structure, I sat down on a small stool by the side of this huge critter, reluctantly put my hands where Papa directed, and holding my breath, tried to make Papa proud.

I pulled and I pumped, but no matter how hard I tried the milk wouldn't flow. Soon the heat and the smell were making me nauseous. Apparently, the victim of my attentions wasn't having fun either. Bellowing loudly, it tried to kick me. Backing cautiously away, I whined, "I can't do it Papa,"

"Sure you can boy," Papa said, "just have faith. With just a little bit of faith you can do anything you set your mind to. Try again."

I did as I was told and tried to have faith. But I still couldn't do it.

Becoming concerned, Papa put on his glasses and took a closer look to see what the problem was. All of a sudden he jumped up, grabbed me by the arm and rushed us out of the barn. "What's wrong Papa?" I asked, thinking he was mad at me for letting him down, "Did I do something wrong?"

Answering quickly as we distanced ourselves from the barnyard, he sounded irritated. "What's wrong with you boy, can't you smell those biscuits? It's time to go in for supper," he said, carefully avoiding my questioning eyes.

Later that evening I overheard one of my uncles explaining to my father what had happened. I didn't learn to milk a cow that day, but I did learn a couple of other things. First, everybody makes some mistakes, even a great man like Papa. And second, no matter how hard you try, no matter how much you have faith, there are some things you can't do. Milking a steer is not in harmony with God's plan. And so my childhood education continued.

Years later, during my early teens, while I was helping Papa work his garden, he asked me what I planned to do with my life.

"I don't know," I answered, "I haven't even thought about it. But I hope I'm a big success like you." Papa was my hero.

"What if I told you a secret that will guarantee you'll be a success, at least in the eyes of God?" Even at that age I knew he considered being a good Christian the only success that was important.

He lay down his hoe and motioned for me to sit by him. He leaned against a fence post, and I leaned against his frail shoulder. "I'm getting old, Raymond. I may not have a chance to tell you this again."

I didn't want to hear about Papa getting old. "Oh, Papa, you're not so ol…"

He put up his hand to hush me. "Just listen to me son, and listen to me carefully"

I knew better than to interrupt again.

"Being a good Christian can be pretty difficult sometimes. You see, God created us but, as we go through our lives, it's up to us to make something worthwhile out of ourselves."

"When we are born, not yet aware we have free will, we are closest to God. As we grow older, and worldlier, we have to make an effort to maintain that relationship. It's hard, but we can do it. We can stay close to God, if we recognize certain realities as a part of God's plan."

"The first reality," Papa said, "is that God created you with free will." I waited for him to continue, but nothing came. I fingered the warm freshly tilled earth where we sat, listened to the buzz of a blue-bottle-fly teasing the wind scrambled silk on a newly ripe ear of corn, and wondered if the other kids had already gone down the hill to swim in the creek.

For a moment I thought Papa had fallen asleep. But he was just thinking and I knew from experience that whatever he told me would be important, even if it did take him a while to get it out.

After what seemed like forever, he finally continued. "God created you," he said, "and you are a unique individual. You are what he wanted you to be, freckles and all. As a child of God you can become whatever you choose to believe in. Your life belongs to you, limited only by your imagination and your faith. You can't change what God created, but you can do with your life what you wish. It's your choice. Isn't that fantastic?"

He closed his eyes again. Papa looked really tired. Just as I started to respond, he continued.

"Raymond," Papa said, "The second reality is, because you have free will, you will become what you think about most." Again I was lost. He explained. "You are the sum total of your thoughts to any given point in your life. Think good thoughts, and you'll be good. Think about success, and you'll be a success. Think loving thoughts and you'll be loved. Think like a Christian, and you'll be a Christian. So select your thoughts carefully." Papa said.

"And the third reality is," Papa said, "God loves you no matter what. So learn to like yourself. Believe you are important in the scheme of God's plan and you will become just that. Accept the fact that God created you for a special reason. God has a purpose for your life."

I heard what Papa said that day, but it was a long time before I understood the truth in what he was saying.

Papa taught me a lot of other things too. One of the most important was just before he died, a few days before my fifteenth birthday. Papa was very sick. He needed blood. I was the only relative available having a blood type compatible with his. My father asked me if I would give a pint of my blood to Papa.

I was scared, but agreed reluctantly. I loved my Papa very much. But Papa loved me even more.

He heard us talking. He knew how much I feared needles. In a feeble whisper we could barely hear, he said, "It isn't necessary for Raymond to give blood. I'm doing just fine." Fortunately, with the encouragement of my father, I agreed and the transfusion was done.

Two weeks later Papa died. A part of me died with him. It hurt so much I wanted to die too. But even in death, Papa was still teaching me. It occurred to me that if Papa could die, I could too. I suddenly became acutely aware of the temporariness of life, realizing fully for the first time that my life here on earth would not go on forever. I vowed to live in a way that Papa would be proud of me.

My high school days were fairly routine. I excelled in sports, got by on my grades, and fell in love with the girl who was later to become my wife. All the time Mama, my maternal grandmother, was telling me what a good boy I was. "So do good", she said. Mother taught me compassion and a passion for order and beauty. And my father set an example of goodness and generosity I could never hope to match.

In college, my first real test of character came, and I'm sorry to say I failed it miserably. I was eighteen years old. I had a football scholarship to Louisiana Tech, a small college in Ruston, Louisiana. I thought I was eager to get on with the season, but the last game in high school I had injured my neck. I never really got over it, and I lost my will to play. So I went from most valuable player in high school to most worthless bench warmer in college.

I blamed God, I blamed fate, and for some reason I blamed everyone and everything but myself. And when nothing else was left I even blamed my parents. I back lashed, rejecting most of the values I really believed to be true. I took the first of many drinks, started running wild, and in general made a fool out of myself. My grades, my reputation, and my feelings about myself took a bad fall. I forgot about what Papa had told me.

But God must have been watching, for in my sophomore year he brought another influential man into my life. I was nineteen years old. He was a Professor of English and a frustrated philosopher. I was a tough jock. I laughed out loud the first time he introduced himself.

Robert Lee Cooper was the quintessential southern gentleman. A century after it was over he was still fighting the civil war. Though heavily biased against those he considered ignorant or lazy, he could still be a charming man to those he decided God had sent to him to save from themselves. Under different circumstances he might have been mistakenly recognized as a confederate colonel or the successful owner and spokesperson for a well known fried chicken franchise.

But he was also a genius. He saw in a minute that I was on the wrong track. He teased and ridiculed me until I started paying attention in his class. He also told me he was going to flunk me out if I didn't get on the stick.

One day he was reading a poem aloud to the class in his eloquent, but off-key voice. A stanza from Thomas Gray's "Elegy in a Country Churchyard."

"Full many a gem of purest ray serene,
The dark unfathomed caves of oceans bear.
And many a flower was born to blush unseen,
And waste it's sweetness on the desert air."

I suddenly realized the poem could have been talking about me. I was wasting the most precious things God had given me. My mind, my youth, my health, my body, and my life in general. That beautiful poem touched my heart. I cried right there in class.

Seeing my need, the professor opened up a whole new world to me. He introduced me to the great minds of the world through carefully selected literature out of his personal library.

Aristotle, he taught me, was known for his Law of Identity. The truth is not relative; things are what they are. You and I are what we are. Socrates introduced the Law of Causality; the principles of cause and effect. For every action there is an equal and opposite reaction. Then there was Plato, remembered for his Principles of Influence; how much one person influences the lives of others. Plato spoke of many ways we are influenced, but even then I considered Influence by Example the most important. I was thinking of my father and Papa.

The professor also insisted I learn and understand the five major areas of philosophy:

Metaphysics, the choice of attitudes toward life. Is life benevolent and good, or is life malevolent and bad?

Epistemology, the study of knowledge or experience. Why we believe what we believe.

Ethics, the values we live by and the principles that result. Honesty, integrity, sincerity.

Politics, the study of authoritarianism versus democracy, control versus freedom.

And finally, what was to become my favorite.

Aesthetics. Art, architecture, the beauty of a sunrise, the quality of life and the environment. The joy of the written word.

It was also during this time that I began to realize I needed a plan for my life. "You've got to have a big dream, if you are going to make a big dream come true," the professor reminded me over and over. He introduced me to the writings of Dale Carnegie and Napoleon Hill, and encouraged me to read and carefully study the *BIBLE*, searching always for passages that promised God's abundance and support.

The Professor got me back on the right track. I went to Louisiana State University to study architecture and pledged myself to excellence. I was in my early twenties. In my fourth year of architectural school, I married my high school sweetheart. It was the best and most important decision I ever made. With her help, support and encouragement school was a breeze. I won a national design award, graduated high in my class, passed my registration exam the first time around, and started my professional career as a designer for a prestigious and award winning architectural firm. Soon I was designing award-winning projects myself.

Everything was moving on schedule and according to plan. I didn't need help from anyone or anything. I was on top of it all. I had expanding career opportunities, a lovely adoring wife, a beautiful daughter, an admiring public and an envious peer group.

But it wasn't enough. I wanted more. So I was always working, always pushing to get more done; to get more. For the good of my family, I rationalized, for my wife and newborn daughter, and of course for me too. One night, coming in long after supper had grown cold and ruined, and after my daughter, without her daddy's hug, had already gone to bed, Pat asked me point blank. "What's the rush? Why do you push so hard?"

It caught me off guard. I thought my priorities were in order. It never occurred to me there was any other way. "Why?" She repeated.

I was surprised by my own answer. "I've got a lot to do. And I don't have much time. Something inside, something inside my head, keeps pushing me."

She looked at me strangely. "You're a young man. You've got plenty of time. Slow down so the rest of us can share it with you."

I promised her I would. But it didn't happen.

The early years of family and career were really good. Too good perhaps, for again I seemed to lose my way. "Success" came too quickly. I began to feel important. I decided "success" was not enough. I wanted wealth and fame. At twenty-eight years old, I abandoned my job, uprooted my family and went back to graduate school on a "hope and a shoestring."

I attended Rice University on a graduate teaching fellowship, got a Master's Degree in Urban Design, wrote an award-winning thesis and published my first book. During that second year in Houston, though our means were meager, it was a time of growth and joy. Many wonderful things happened, but the greatest was the arrival of our son Robert, a miracle of survival through God's grace and the unwavering faith of his mother that he would be mentally whole in spite of an extremely troubled birth. Our family complete, we had each other and the promise of God filled lives ahead of us.

After graduation I restarted my career, joint ventured in a real estate development company, and soon thereafter became vice president of a conglomerate architectural, landscape architectural and graphic design company. A year later I started my own companies specializing in these areas.

Then the opportunity of a lifetime. Vice president of research, design and marketing, with a generous salary, bonuses, benefits and stock options in the largest home building and real estate development company in the richest small community in all of rural Texas. Green acres in suburbia in close proximity to the Gulf.

Our new home would be in Lake Jackson, fifty miles south of Houston and six miles from the sunny Gulf of Mexico. It was founded as a new town by the Dow Chemical Company in the early nineteen forties in response to their need to locate near the Gulf where they could mine magnesium for manufacturing munitions for the war. Built on the Abner Jackson Sugar Plantation, a beautiful place partially covered with old growth forest, centuries old oak trees, and surrounding an oxbow lake, a cut off of the Brazos River, Lake Jackson offered the perfect location for Dow executives and engineers to live.

All was going well, and as I had planned. Approaching thirty-three years of age, I was on top of the world. I was Raymond Burroughs, the great American hope. All I had to do was smile and anything I wanted was there for the taking.

Then it all changed. Out of the blue, on my thirty-third birthday, I found myself asking another surprising question. "Christ was crucified when he was thirty-three; I wonder what will happen to me?" God knowing must have been saddened...

A screeching of tires put me almost against the windshield. Thank God for seat belts. Pat, knuckles white, had a death grip on the steering wheel. A couple of teen-agers on skateboards, playing chicken, had raced across our driveway just as she was turning in. Seeing Pat bury her head in her hands they laughed and flapped their arms, unaware of what a close call they had just had.

Pat looked up with tears in her eyes. "Are you all right?"

"Kids," I replied, "they think they're bulletproof. If only they knew."

Priorities

Time is the hunter
Life is the game.
Hunter and hunted
Are one and the same.

Deciding what to do with your last remaining days is not an easy task. Though Pat and I agreed spending time with our immediate family should be our first priority, there were still some hard choices to be made. Time was running out and we were both becoming very particular about how we spent the minutes, the hours and the days of the life we had left to share.

It was one of my favorite times of the year, primarily because it wasn't long until the Whitewing Dove hunting season opened in Mexico. My friends and I had a lease on a ranch near Lake Guerro that offered wing shooting unrivaled by few locations in North America. Each year I looked forward to making the opening day hunt. Not being able to do so was a painful reminder that there were a lot of things that weren't going to be done before my time was up.

But I guess it was in God's plan that my "last hunt" was meant to be. As soon as word got out I wasn't able to make the trip to Mexico a friend I hadn't hunted with in several years called and invited me to join him on a Mourning Dove hunt. It would be a short trip. His father's farm wasn't far from where we lived. He said the fields were full of maize and the birds were there in droves.

At first I said no. There were greater priorities. But Pat, knowing how much I loved to hunt, encouraged me to go. There were things she needed to do, she said, and we both needed a break.

When we arrived at the farm, I wondered if I had made the right decision in agreeing to come along. It almost seemed unreal. There we were, two macho buddies, trying to pretend life was great and looking forward to just another beautiful afternoon in the field. Both of us were doing everything we could to avoid discussing what was really on our minds.

About a hundred yards from the truck, my friend stopped, surveyed the area and pointed toward a stand of cottonwoods along a ditch on the far side of the maize covered field. He could tell I was preoccupied but pretended to ignore it. "You take a stand here by the fence and I'll move to that row of trees and see if I can move some birds your way."

I shook my head. Funny what you think about when your world is falling in. I remembered a newsreel I had seen at the movies when I was a kid. It showed President Eisenhower in a duck blind watching as two mallard ducks flared up from the marsh in front of him. Like a true sportsman he stood, took the perfect swing, and downed them both with two shots from his twelve gauge automatic. Then the camera pulled back, showing a wider view. Squatting in the reeds just out of shotgun range in front of the president were two secret service agents with a wire cage full of mallards, waiting for the signal to release the next pair.

I guess the President was short on time too. Now it was my turn for a canned hunt.

"Hey, that's all right," I said. Let's both wait here until the birds start to fly."

"It's getting late," he said, "We don't have much time."

I looked down to avoid his eyes.

"Raymond, what I meant…"

I forced a laugh. Everything about time had a double meaning those days. I slapped him with my hat.

"Thanks for the reminder—friend. You always were the subtle one. Remember that time your wife found you passed out in the back of the truck. You told her you had fallen asleep waiting for me to drive you home. She believed you until she saw you didn't have any pants on."

"Hey, I was framed. You and Harold…."

"Never mind," I laughed, this time sincere, "Never mind. You're right. Time's a wasting. Just go drive the birds."

"Alright, alright, I'm going."

He wandered off toward the trees mumbling…."Darn prima donna…"

I leaned against a fence post and began to watch for the birds. Sure enough the biggest swarm of Mourning doves I had ever seen swooped across the field toward me. Shotgun to shoulder, I swung with their flight. But I didn't fire. Another flight passed low overhead. This time I didn't even lift my gun.

A few minutes later, my hunting buddy, stumbling out of breath, followed not far behind. Even before he got to me he was shouting. "Hey. What's wrong with you? Couldn't you see those birds? They passed right over you."

"Yeah, I know. It's getting late. Let's go." I said, not realizing how harshly I must have sounded.

Knowing something was wrong, he said nothing more on the long walk to the truck. About halfway there, I turned to him and handed him my shotgun. "Here, take this. I won't need it anymore." He could see I was serious.

"Hey. What are you talking about? We'll come out here next weekend and I guarantee I'll put some birds so close even a sorry shot like you can't miss."

"No, no. I want you to have it. It's the one my father gave to me."

"Raymond. Give me a break. I don't know what to say."

"Don't say anything. Just put it in the truck before I decide to use it on myself."

We got in the truck and were on our way. The sun was just settling below the tree line. A large flight of water birds silhouetted against the dimming sky drifted silently across the road ahead. They were going home too. It was dark before my good friend, patiently curious to that point, finally broke the silence.

"Raymond. How come you let those birds go by back there? You could have had your limit in fifteen minutes."

It was a long moment before I was able to answer.

"Waiting for those birds out there got me to thinking about dying again. Obviously I've been doing a lot of that lately. I've about decided the physical part's not going to be that bad. Probably like going to sleep and waking up in a better place. I've also realized I'm not afraid to die, but it does seem unfair. I haven't had time to do all the living I planned to do yet."

"That's why I came down from Houston so we could make this hunt, isn't it?" he questioned, not so sure anymore.

"Yeah, but when those birds flew over, it occurred to me that maybe they hadn't had time to do all the living they planned to do either. Or maybe, since the shoe is on the other foot, I just don't have the stomach for killing anymore. You know better than anyone, I've been a bird hunter all my life. I must have killed ten thousand doves. And never once did I think of those birds as anything but targets. But today, for some reason they were just too beautiful to shoot. Just flying through the air, minding their own business, above all the troubles and pain of the world, totally oblivious to the fact that something or someone might come along and end it all."

"They're just animals, Raymond. Even the Bible says they were put here for the enjoyment of man."

"I know," I said wearily, "but since this thing came up I've been doing a lot of thinking. Life is truly a miracle, a gift from God. It's much, much too precious to be cut short without a reason. Today when I saw those birds, all I wanted to do was live and let live."

Grieving Then Hope

All dreams are gray at night
But then there comes the light
And shadows' fears are quickly speared
With rays of hope and sight.

The nightmares were frightening, full of darkness and shadows, and a perpetual chase with time running out. Waking up was a welcome relief. Morning seemed familiar but everything had changed. The world as I knew it would never again be the same. Almost a week had passed since we had been to Houston.

I lay quietly, soaking up the wonders of being alive. The sun was shining through the crack in the curtains. It seemed brighter than usual. I heard birds beyond the window, their songs more beautiful than ever. I pulled up the sheet, noticing the smell of its freshness. I felt great, acutely aware of the softness of my pillow and the texture of warm fabrics against my skin.

I heard Pat in the kitchen talking on the telephone. The sense of awareness vanished, replaced by a dull ache somewhere deep in my head. I closed my eyes and pulled the covers higher around my shoulders. I wanted to hide. Learning you are going to die is something that happens in books, or movies, but always to someone else. The idea that my life might end soon was incomprehensible; unacceptable. I felt betrayed, cheated, deceived and even ashamed as the magnitude of reality again sank home.

It was true. I was finished, a failure in the eyes of all whom loved and cared about me. How would I face my remaining days with the woman I was deserting? I needed time to think, to find a way to tell her how much I truly loved her, and time to reassure her that she and the kids would be okay and provided for after I was gone. It was new territory for me. Thinking about dying isn't something you normally do when you're in your early thirties.

"Just a minute Howard, I'll get him on," I heard her say. She had talked to Howard several times since we were in Houston, but never asked me to join in the conversation.

"What now?" I wondered out loud.

Hearing her coming down the hall, I wanted to run away. Too late. She was sitting on the edge of the bed leaning down to kiss me. And she was smiling. "We've found that miracle. Howard found a doctor that can help us." She had to tell me several times before I understood. In a conversation with an associate, Howard had learned of a neurosurgeon in California who had developed a technique of microsurgery that allowed him to operate around sensitive nerves where others could not. His name was Ed Morris. "Great risk," Howard had said, "but a shred of hope."

Howard arranged a conference call. After explaining to the doctor what we were up against, he put me on.

"Dr. Morris. This is Raymond Burroughs."

"How's it going Raymond?"

"Not so good. Dr. Lowe tells me you might be able to help."

"Sometimes we can. He explained your situation. Why don't we schedule for you to come out here right after the first of the year?"

"But…"

"My schedule stays pretty full. Usually takes about ninety days to work someone in. Usually takes a few weeks just to pretest."

"But…"

"By then I'll be back from Europe. Going over to get married. To Miss Sweden. We're going to tour the continent.

Take a six-week honeymoon." By that time it was obvious he was already in another world. "Did you see her in the MISS WORLD pageant? Talk about a knockout. I may be getting too old for this sort of…"

"Dr. Morris!" I shouted. "By the time you get back I'll be dead." I slammed down the phone; fully aware I might have just missed what might have been my only chance to survive. I ran into the bedroom and slammed the door. Pat didn't follow. She understood me like no one else in the world. Sometimes I needed support. Sometimes I just needed to be left alone.

Left to myself for the first time in several days, I found my thoughts dwelling not on my death, but rather on the prospect of losing my life, and in turn all that seemed truly important to me at that point.

Things precious become more valuable when discovered about to be lost. It is said the memories of a drowning man flash before his eyes in his last conscious moments. This might be true, but once I realized I might be going to die, it was those things not yet experienced that dominated my thoughts and whose poten- tial loss grieved me most. There were so many wonderful things I had intended to do. But like most people, forgetting that life could suddenly end, I had continually put them off.

For the next few hours I found myself grieving for things I knew could never be. Many were clearly beyond the scope of my remaining days. The continuation of a "successful" career, the opportunity to make a significant contribution to the wel- fare of my fellow men, the promise of shared accomplishments with a maturing family, and a number of other experiences that make up the memories of a life fully lived, all seemed painfully out of reach.

One area of my life was particularly disturbing. I found little that documented I indeed had lived a Christian life. Sure I tried to obey the Ten Commandments and live by the Golden Rule. But beyond that I could not recall one time where my being a Christian had influenced the lives of others.

Since a child I had been a professed Christian, but like many others I had somehow rationalized that attainment first of my personal and family goals was essential if I was to have the time and resources to make a worthwhile Christian contribution. I also mistakenly assumed that being relatively young I had a very long life ahead of me. I let my priorities get out of order. It was my mistake, my choice. And I had no one to blame but myself.

At that eleventh hour, I had a lot of time to think about choices. I also thought a lot about God. And Christ.

Christ had a choice how he would spend His life. Even facing death on the cross He still had a choice. Fortunately for us, He chose to give up his life to pay for our sins. Christ always made the right choice. By doing so He gave us a choice as to how we will spend eternity. All He asks of us is that we too, make the right decision and follow Him.

Looking back now, it seems amazing that it took such a serious threat to my life for me to realize just how much the choice offered by Christ truly means. Because of Him, though I might be going to die, I didn't have to worry about where I would spend eternity. In spite of my shortcomings, I had the promise of eternal life.

Later much later, I decided to rejoin the family, determined more than ever to get in as much living as possible during the time I had left. There was much to be done, but most important was the need to love and spend time with my family, building memories not for myself, but for those that would remain once I was no longer a part of this world. There was much to be said, much to be shared and much to be savored. And much to be understood that was beyond understanding.

After an evening of clarity, of seeing Pat, Ramona, and Rob like I had never seen them before, hanging on every word, every moment and hoping the evening would never end, I went to bed with a prayer. It was a prayer of thanksgiving, a prayer for courage, a prayer of acceptance, and a prayer not for me, but for the welfare of my family. Somehow, even then, the only prayer that seemed to work, to bring the comfort and hope I was so much searching for, was to pray for God's will to be done.

The dreams were still there, but kinder and gentler that night. With first consciousness, like the last wisp of morning fog over the gentle gurgle of a cold running river, remnants of the dream seemed as real as the coming day. I had traveled on an endless journey to a timeless place, of peace and beauty and song, and then just before I woke, I realized I had gone full circle, arriving once again at my home. With outreached arms Pat and the children were welcoming me.

I lingered a moment, trying to understand. But I couldn't of course. The meaning and purpose of a dream, like life, is as elusive as the rise ring of a trout in fast moving water. Sometimes we think we catch a glimpse of it, but we're never really sure what we saw.

Moments later I was fully awake. Refreshed by the first good night's sleep in a long time, I was acutely aware of the present, looking forward to sharing another precious day with my family. At breakfast Pat seemed more herself too. Lost in our own thoughts, we were enjoying the quiet before the kids woke up.

The telephone shattered the silence, startling us both. Pat got there first. It was Howard. He had Dr. Morris on a conference call. I raced for the bedroom phone.

"Raymond, Ed Morris here. Got a package this morning. The special microscopes I ordered almost two years ago. The Dutch may be slow, but they make the best optical instruments in the world. Custom all the way, exactly to my specifications.

I'm anxious to try them out. Think you can be out here the first of next week?"

"Out here" was Pasadena, California. His offices were just across the street from Huntington Memorial Hospital where he treated private patients. He was also Head of Neurosurgery at the University of Southern California. A long ways from Lake Jackson, Texas, and even further from our hometown of birth, Shreveport, Louisiana.

"Yes sir, thank you, we'll be there," I blurted out. Then in a state of bewilderment, overcome with emotion, I hung up the phone.

Fortunately, Pat and Howard stayed on. There were a lot of details to be worked out.

My mind was reeling. God's plan was in full swing. What were the odds that those instruments would arrive a day after we first called? What were the odds Dr. Morris would postpone the wedding? What were the odds that Dr. Morris would decide to use the new equipment to help me and call back? What were the odds that, because of the wedding plans, Dr. Morris's schedule, normally full for months at a time, would be immediately open?

It took me a while to accept the truth, but it was there all along. With God on my side, the odds were not only good; they were very good indeed.

Departing

Now at once life slips away
Maybe soon is yesterday
Hours flee, tides run low
Lights grow dim and we must go.

During the period immediately prior to that critical operation, we learned that, though relatively new in the community, we were not alone at all. I systematically went about getting my affairs in order. I had a local attorney draw up a will, located the critical papers that documented our financial security and worldly goods and organized them so Pat would know how to continue should I not be there to help her in the future. In a moment of insanity, I even cancelled a couple of magazine subscriptions. I also visited my many business associates and advised them of the situation. Few understood the magnitude of what we were up against.

But many did care. It had been less than six months since we moved from Houston to Lake Jackson, Texas - a small town where people know and care about what happens to their neighbors. In a matter of hours after our dilemma became common knowledge the phone and the doorbell were ringing constantly. People from our neighborhood, members of local churches, business associates, community leaders and many others took the time to care about and support us in an outpouring of love and compassion we could never have anticipated. People we hardly knew were bringing meals to the house, wishing us well, and promising their support through their prayers.

One of our biggest concerns was what to do with our children, Ramona, 8, and Robert, 3. The doctor's staff told us we should plan to be gone for at least two or three months. Especially if I should survive the operation. Recovery and rehabilitation could take considerable time, they said.

What were we going to do?

Oh ye of little faith, I recall admonishing myself a few days later. I should have known God had a plan for taking care of our family too.

A few months before we had invited Pat's mother to come live with us. She had been ill, and we were going to take care of her. Now, through the Grace of God, she had recovered. In her best health since Ernest had died, she was ready, willing and thought she was able to take care of her grandchildren. But she wasn't young anymore, we knew, and the kids were a handful, even to Pat and me. We wondered if she could do it alone.

We soon learned she wouldn't have to. A man from our church I had only recently met in my business dealings came to our home to meet my mother-in-law and assure all of us he would be coming by on a daily basis to check on things while we were gone. Several local doctors offered to help out should she or the children need medical assistance. Others told us, no matter what happened, when we got back, there would be new and exciting career opportunities waiting should I need a new start. Our preacher at that time came by on a regular basis and just sat and talked, confirming for both of us that my religious beliefs were in order. We prayed together that God's will be done. He read to me from the Bible. "All things work together for those that love God."

In spite of all these assurances, we needed more courage, more stamina, and more faith than we could ever muster by ourselves. Once again, the answer came through prayer. Joined by those of others in our community, from our hometown where we grew up and finally from across the nation and a worldwide network of prayer, it soon became apparent that the Bible promises were true. God would respond to our needs on a moment by moment basis.

It is impossible to communicate how important Christian support was in preparing us for the ordeal we were about to face. I alone had to go under the knife. And Pat, alone in a strange city and far from home, would have to deal with the uncertainty of the surgery and the future, the separation from her husband and children, and the agony of a soul mate whose other half is hurting or in harm's way. But we knew we would never be truly alone. God would be there. And our fellow Christians, his earthbound angels, would be there too.

Those last few days before we left for California were a blur. And, like so many other things at the height of that period of chaos, remains so in my memory today. What I do remember is the urgency with which we lived, the speed with which the days passed, and the exhausting length of those sleepless nights. We were grasping to hold on to life as we had known it up to that point, fully aware that change, major and devastating change, was on its way. We knew, and we knew we knew, but were equally determined to avoid admitting, that there was nothing we could do but pray to stop the inevitable, or for that matter, even slow it. But we tried.

Dreams of tomorrow and far off places became insignificant as the preciousness of the moments, limited in supply, suddenly extended their value to overflow our days. The sun settled slower, for the memory was etched in our brains, and the bird songs seem clearer, for our hearts heard not only their song, but also their sadness or cheer. And all about the small became great and those things once deemed so important graciously yielded to the glory of the most basic of realities, the joy of family and the presence of God in our lives.

During the day and late into the evenings we loved like we had never loved before. We cared about and for each other like we had never cared before. We played with our children like we had never played before. And we held on to all that was dear or seemed dear for as long as we could. We pretended life was normal, all the time wondering who we were trying to convince.

In the darkness of our bedroom, after we had kissed good-night, even while Pat and I continued to hold each other, we turned to our secret thoughts, avoiding all discussion of what was to come. It was not an act of denial, but rather one of kindness, a futile effort by each of us to spare the other the pain and frustration we were feeling.

In the daylight we prayed aloud and together. In the darkness we prayed silently and alone. But always, no matter when it was, where we were, or what we were doing, there was an overriding and continuous prayer in our consciousness. Our prayer was not to circumvent the pending surgery, for even with miracles it seemed inevitable that removal of the tumor was essential if there was to be any hope of extending my life. Our prayer was for hope, strength, courage, faith, and that God's will be done.

As individuals, our prayers were not for ourselves, but for each other and the ones we loved who would be affected by the outcome of the surgery. I can honestly say, after that moment on the beach when I first discovered the tumor, I was never afraid of dying. However, I was afraid for my wife and children, should I die, or perhaps worse, survive in an altered or compromised state of mental and physical consciousness that would do nothing but extend their misery or make me a lifelong burden on them.

When the day finally arrived that Pat and I were to leave for California, I had to tell Ramona and Rob goodbye, knowing in my heart that it might be for the last time. It was one of the most painful moments I have ever experienced, before, during or after the surgery. But they were brave, and we were brave, and somehow we managed to leave without a major outburst. But even with the conviction that we had God's support, I cried all the way to the Houston airport.

From the outset of the crisis we had made every effort to shelter our innocent children from the reality of the situation. Now, as we were about to depart, I wondered if too much had been left unsaid. Rob, almost four, was obviously too young to understand, but Ramona, almost nine, was very mature for her age. Maybe if we had trusted her to understand, I could have told her how much the thought of leaving them, perhaps forever, was breaking my heart. Perhaps, I prayed, she would understand that anyway. And when the time was right, she could convince Rob too.

The simplest things become very difficult when the stakes are high. Over those past few days endless discussions had taken place on what was the best way for us to get to Houston Intercontinental Airport for our flight to California. Since Ines had her car to use while we were gone, we could have taken our car and left it in a commercial lot if we were willing to pay the fees for an indefinite period of time. Considering everything, that didn't seem practical.

Friends had offered to drive us, but knowing both the departure and the trip would be very emotional, I ruled that out right away.

"We need to be alone. I need to be alone. What might prove to be our last moments together," I told Pat, "are far too precious to share." Maybe I was selfish. It never occurred to me that the she or the others might have benefited from the support.

Taking a limousine was not acceptable either. "Too much like a funeral procession," I said. Seeing the hurt in Pat's eyes, I regretted my sarcasm the moment I spoke. Sometimes in moments of weakness, I forgot how much she was hurting too.

After much discussion, we settled on a rental car. It made sense, even to my clouded mind. We could turn it in at the airport, there would be no parking fees, and it didn't matter how long we would be gone.

Then, much too soon, it was time to be on our way. We finished loading the car. Deep in thought about the surrealistic situation, it was all I could do to focus on what we were doing. At the other end of the walk, my beautiful daughter and unquestioning son stood much too quietly by the front door of our house, hand in hand with their grandmother. The presence of the rental car alone was probably enough to tip them off that something was very unusual, perhaps very wrong, about that morning's goodbye.

Suddenly, as if aware of the urgency of the situation, Ramona turned loose of her grandmother's hand and raced along the walk. Forcing a smile that melted my heart, her golden bouncing hair a highlighted halo in the morning sun, she floated like an angel toward me.

Forcing back the tears, I saw her as I might never live to see her again, not just a child but the promise of the woman to be, a beautiful woman like her mother; wise, warm, tender and always putting others before herself. She seemed much too mature for her age.

When she leapt into my arms, I almost went down. Arms around my neck, she clung to me for what seemed like an eternity.

"Don't go daddy," she said, as she had said so many times before. But this time it had new meaning. And I knew she knew. I kneeled down and hugged her tightly.

After a long moment she finally stepped back. There were no tears in her eyes, but the look was a question, an accusation, and a plea all at once. I thought I would die on the spot. I felt like I was deserting her, that too much had been left unsaid, and that I should have told her the truth and trusted her to understand that no matter what happened to me my love would be with her forever. But now it was too late, and for fear of upsetting her further, nothing more was said.

The next thing I knew, Robert was there too, our miracle child, energy in action.

I hugged them both for a long time, probably longer than I should have, considering we were trying so hard to protect them.

I told them I loved them, that they should mind their grandmother, and that we would be back soon. Then, at Pat's insistence that we needed to be on our way, they were gone from my embrace, turning about to tell her goodbye. Feeling like a man without a soul, I hugged Ines, patted both kids on the head, and about to break down, retreated into the car.

Soon Pat was by my side, being strong as always, but suffering silently as we waved goodbye. The last thing I saw as we drove away was Robert running across the yard toward the car, with Ramona close behind trying to stop him from running into the street. Ines too was trying to keep up. For a brief moment I forgot about my own troubles and worried about someone else. Ines, all alone, was going to have her hands full with those two while we were gone. Any woman would. Even their mother, I remember thinking.

As she had for the past several weeks, Pat was driving. And this time I hadn't argued. There were too many unknowns about what effect the tumor might have on me. For all we knew I might pass out, have a stroke, or for that matter die while we were on the road.

"No sense both of us getting killed," I had finally agreed when Pat suggested she drive. Besides, we both realized, I would be too distracted to concentrate on driving.

Feeling a temporary sense of relief at finally being on our way, I turned to get something out of the back seat. It was then I noticed the small plastic photo and music cube on the back floorboard. When it was wound up, it played "Speak Softly Love", heart rending music from the movie "Love Story." A going away gift from the kids, it held five Polaroid photos selected from the many we had taken a few days before during an early celebration of Robert's birthday. He would be four on October 6, three days before my surgery was to take place. The pictures were Pat's idea of one way all of our immediate family could be at least visibly with us while we were in California

To others those photos might have seemed ordinary, but to me, facing the prospect of death, all that I loved, all that really mattered, was there for me to remember and cherish. There was Ramona in her pretty blue dress, swinging and laughing, as always, melting my heart; Robert, as proud as I had ever seen him, with a smile as wide as the sky, surrounded by his early birthday presents, holding an American flag; the four of us by the swing set, me looking healthy and fit, arm around my beautiful Pat with Ramona and Robert close in front sitting in the swings; Pat sitting in the grass with Robert on her lap while Ramona snuggled with our puppy, laughing as he licked her face. And finally, Robert and his grandmother sitting on the couch in the house looking much too serious for the moment.

When I bumped the cube, it sounded a single note. Hearing my breath catch, Pat reached over and gave me a reassuring pat on the shoulder. That was all it took. I totally lost control. The dam broke. I cried and I cried, like an abandoned child lost in the night who knows he will never see his loved ones again.

For a couple who hadn't traveled much, especially by air, California seemed far away. When we boarded the plane, Pat insisted I take the window seat. Partly, I think, because she wanted to shield me from unnecessary conversation with strangers who couldn't have had a clue of what was going on in my head, but also because she knew how much I needed psychological space. My normally limited tolerance for small talk was rapidly approaching zero. In spite of my struggle to keep the faith, time and reality seemed to be closing in on me.

For most of that flight, high above the clouds, the earth far below, it seemed I was suspended in time somewhere between heaven and earth, far from the reality I had always known. It was a time of quiet contemplation, of serious consideration of where I had been and where I might be going.

My thoughts were of life, and death, and life after death. And about the miracles that had gotten me to that point in my journey. Ever since I accepted Christ as my Savior, I have truly believed that everything that happens, either directly or indirectly, plays a part in God's plan for the eternal salvation of mankind. Don't misunderstand. I don't think God gave me the tumor. That would be predestination. What I do believe is that once I had the tumor, God showed me the way to handle the crisis, and in time allowed me to realize that even something so life changing could be used to positive advantage.

Even though I thought I might be going to die, I still believed in miracles. More firmly than ever, based on what had already happened since we learned of the tumor. The more obvious ones kept going through my head.

1. The tumor was discovered in time to do something.
2. I bumped the door frame on the way out of the doctor's office.
3. He noticed and arranged for more test.
4. My car got stuck up to the axle in the sand on that lonely beach.

5. I forgot about it and drove free without a second thought.
6. Moments before I had turned my destiny over to God.
7. We called on Pat's lifelong friend for medical advice.
8. A state of the art x-ray machine had just arrived in Houston.
9. Our friend was the radiologist who operated it.
10. Our friend located a neurosurgeon in California who specialized in critical cases.
11. He wouldn't be available for six months. He was getting married.
12. I said I would be dead by then and hung up. I had less than six weeks.
13. Specialized optical instruments, several years in the making, arrived the next day.
14. The doctor called back, anxious to try them. He cancelled his wedding.
15. Due to the wedding plans, his schedule was clear. He offered to help.
16. Our kids would have to stay behind. We'd be gone for months.
17. Pat's mother had come to live with us because she was alone and ill.
18. She had quickly recovered and could take care of our children.
19. We had just moved from a large indifferent city to a small town that cared.
20. People we had only recently met offered to help look after our family.
21. Others contacted their California friends to help look after Pat and me.

The fact I was thirty-three, the same age Christ was when He was crucified, was also constantly on my mind. Especially since the greatest miracle of all time was the resurrection and the promise of eternal life.

Christ chose to give up his life to pay for my sins. And in doing He gave me a choice as to how I will spend eternity. And all He had asked in return was that I accept Him as my Savior. Thanks to my Christian upbringing, I had made that choice many years before.

Facing the threat of death, the choice offered by Christ took on new dimensions. Not only did I know Christ would be with me wherever this fateful journey might lead, I also knew I had the promise of eternal life should my earthly life come to an end.

That afternoon, when the wheels of the plane touched the ground, I realized my journey had just begun. The question, I thought, would soon be answered. Life or death?

Obviously, it never occurred to me it might be both.

A Rough Beginning

Dreams shared of mystic lands
Time to ponder, moments grand
Loved ones near, God filled goals
Life so sure, so warm and whole
Days of joy, nights of sorrow
Endless prayers, all for tomorrow.

If empathy could be captured on canvas, it would be a painting of Dr. Morris's eyes the first time we saw him. Though small in stature, the caring, the calmness, and the confidence that seemed to radiate from his gaze, captured our hearts and buoyed our hopes. The first time he shook my hand, though his was small in my own, I sensed at once that the gentle strength of his grip was more than that of a surgeon. It was the grip of a healer, of one who could deliver what he knew from experience he dare not promise.

Older than he looked, around fifty-five or sixty I guessed at the time, he had heavily grayed hair, chiseled features, a darkly tanned face, and deep crevasses of concern radiating from the corners of his eyes. Though slightly stooped at the shoulders, probably a result of the focus required by the close and critical nature of the surgeries he performed and built like a professional tennis player or fitness trainer, Dr. Morris had a lightness of step and quickness of movement that suggested he loved and lived life to its fullest.

When he spoke to me, his attention was so acute I knew at once we would soon become friends. It was as though my wellbeing was the most important consideration in his life. Driving toward the Pacific much later in the day, Pat told me she sensed the same positive energy when he turned his attention to her. There was no doubt in either of our minds. God's will was unfolding before us. Here was the neurosurgeon that was to be God's instrument in saving my life.

After a few minutes of introduction to Dr. Morris's staff, confirmation that we were comfortable with our room at the Hilton, where Pat would be alone once I was in the hospital, and assurances by the doctor's staff that Pat would be looked after while I was out of commission, the conversation quickly turned to the medical business at hand. With less than forty-eight hours remaining before the operation to remove the tumor, there was a lot to be done. And understood. After a brief physical, a few tests of my balance, confirmation I was fully deaf in my left ear, and a general explanation of what we could expect over the next two days, the conversation began to focus on our psychological well being.

It seemed most important to Dr. Morris to impress on both Pat and me the potential impact of the medical ordeal that was about to befall us. Several times during that conversation he paused to question whether we understood or not. He was concerned by the calm, almost matter-of-fact way we were accepting his state-ment that death on the operating table was a possible out-come of the surgery. Death or worse were the words he used.

Pat and I just nodded, and said we understood. There was no way he could know that the peace he saw on the outside merely reflected God's strength we felt on the inside. We were scared, and the fact that we might soon be separated by death made us feel sad, but we also knew that God was on our side, and regardless of what happened, we would sooner or later be together again.

At some point that afternoon, reality began to become sur-real. I began to block out what seemed like small talk, focusing instead on the seemingly endless stack of paperwork that had to be signed before we could even begin to embark on a medical venture of such magnitude. I remember little of what was being said during that late hour, but I do remember signing paper after paper, probably releases of liability and acknowledgements of what might result from my "voluntary" decision to go forward with the surgery. I didn't read or care what I was signing; legal issues didn't seem a very high priority at the time.

When the paperwork was done we were anxious to be on our way. During a moment of self-pity on the flight earlier in the day, I had sarcastically said something about at least getting to see the Pacific before I died. Holding back the tears, Pat had promised we would see it together. "Before and after the opera-tion," she had whispered quietly. I'm not sure whether she was trying to convince herself or me.

Just before we left the doctor's office, we were told where to go and what to do on the following morning when I was to have my final angiogram at Los Angeles County Hospital. Dr. Morris said the films made in Houston were clear, but more recent and detailed information was essential if the neu-rosurgery was to have any possibility of a positive outcome. What he didn't say, or at least dwell on, was the physical and psychological devastation that would result from the intrave-nous chemicals to be used in the angiogram. In spite of the confidence eroding experiences of the past few months, I still thought I was tough. Little did I know.

Finally on our own again with about two hours of daylight left, while I gave directions from a totally outdated map, Pat head-ed the rental car south on the Harbor Freeway. Passing Elysian Park, downtown Los Angeles and the Civic Center, we exited onto Wilshire Boulevard, a congested, winding thoroughfare that ran westward about twenty miles toward Santa Monica before ending at the Pacific Ocean

It didn't take long to realize that what my Urban Design professors at Rice had said was true as we compared Los Angeles to Houston and other major cities. Trapped in endless suburbia, in traffic creeping forward with the momentum of a slow moving parking lot, another precious day was quickly slipping away. "Los Angeles is the only city in the world" one of them had quoted from a bedraggled 1945 issue of *The Saturday Evening Post*, "where you can drink in a drive-in saloon, eat in a cafe shaped like a toad, and they will bury you in a 'Happy Cemetery.'"

The professors were right. Los Angeles was clearly a city built without a plan. As we approached and crossed over and beyond the southern edge of Hollywood, discotheques and psychedelic shops stood side by side with expensive boutiques and restaurants. Mammoth sized billboards promoting the stars, famous restaurants, and Hollywood nightspots lined both sides of the streets, hiding small bungalows and businesses, tired remnants of another, perhaps quieter time of long before. I found it hard to imagine as we passed through that suburban squalor that only a short distance away was Sunset Boulevard with its famous Sunset Strip, Hollywood and Vine, and other lavish locations known throughout the world. The cities of Beverly Hills, West Hollywood, and Bel Air, historic home communities of the stars were the birthplaces and sometimes current locations of many of the colossal movie studios, Twentieth Century Fox, Warner Brothers, Columbia Pictures, Paramount Studios, and myriads of others lesser known Hollywood establishments.

In spite of the traffic most of the drive passed pleasantly enough. With Pat driving I could study and comment on the old and new architecture to my heart's content. As the evening cooled, we rolled down the windows and turned up the radio. Turning south on the last leg of our trip our worries were momentarily forgotten as Barbara Streisand began crooning one of my favorite songs, *The Way We Were*.

Our relief was short lived as the blinding light of the late afternoon sun, reflecting off the sculptured glass wall of a newly completed building complex, forced us back to the reality of our situation. We were running out of time, in more ways than one. Trapped in an endless mire of cars and trucks, it began to appear we were not going to make it to the coast before dark.

I was surprised that we did. Arriving at the coast just before sunset, we got out of the car and stood arm in arm by the edge of the Pacific Ocean, watching quietly spellbound, as the largest sun one could ever imagine settled slowly out of sight below the rounded horizon of a gradually silvering sea, undeniable documentation of the inevitable and irreversible nature of the passing of time. My heart sank with it, heavy with the realization that another irretrievable day had passed.

I knelt down in the sand and touched the water; glad it was getting dark. I lowered my head hoping Pat, standing behind, would not see my tears; an unstoppable flow like the surging of the surf they dripped slowly from my face into the thin fingers of the soon retreating tide. Though significant to me, they made no visible impact on the surface of the water. In an instant, not a dimple or a trace remained to record they had ever existed. A parable of my life to that point, I thought, knowing in my heart that those tears would have about as much impact on the salinity or volume of the ocean as my life had had during my time here on earth.

Of course Pat wasn't fooled, but she was kind. Stepping up behind to help me to my feet, she put her arms around my waist and pulled me close. We stood quietly watching as full darkness fell across that boundless expanse. A cooling sea breeze began, calming my heart as it dried my cheeks. Finally regaining my composure, I turned about and kissed Pat gently, grateful again for the time we still had to share. I was suddenly engulfed by an overwhelming sadness. How could it be, I wondered, that a love so great might soon come to an end?

A short time later we were somewhere down the coast, seated in a romantic restaurant in Marina Del Rey, in a cozy candle-lit booth with a huge expanse of glass overlooking the bay. Yachts swayed lazily at their moorings, lights glistened brightly, their reflections rising and falling with the swells, an occasional seagull swooped by, and all about were the sounds of life and joy.

The seafood was excellent, the service was good, and almost every moment made a memory to be savored. Pat, blond hair glowing like a halo around her angelic face, was radiant. Thank you Lord, I remember whispering in my mind, for this small part of heaven on earth.

After dinner we walked around the complex, visiting one specialty shop after another, trying to hold onto that very special evening. But time wouldn't stop, and the ventures of tomorrow were coming our way all too fast. We headed back to the hotel, silent with our own thoughts for most of the way. Though confronted with the heavy burden of uncertainty and an early awakening, we loved in silent desperation, then holding each other closely, talked late into the night, each of us, out of consideration of the other, being careful not to mention it might be our last chance.

The following morning began with a start and continued with a stressful rush until we reached the hospital. In a bad part of town, it was enclosed like a fortress, with a guard to greet us as soon as we drove through the gates. As prearranged, we parked in the staff parking lot.

Soon we were escorted to our floor, I kissed Pat goodbye, and I was quickly escorted to the prep area. All too soon I was lying under a sheet in the surgery suite fully awake with a small needle in my thigh just below my groin. Dr. Morris was there, hardly recognizable behind his mask. Inserting a small tube in my leg was a radiologist I had not met before. There was little pain, but it was weird watching the monitor suspended above as a thin line eased up my leg, extended into and past my heart and finally came to rest somewhere in the lower part of my brain.

Whether it was fear or the cold metal surface of the table where I lay that made me tremble I'm not sure, but there was a period there when I thought I would vibrate off the table.

Finally the moment of reckoning arrived. The radiologist began to administer the first dose of chemicals. "Brace yourself," he said, "you'll feel a burning sensation that sometimes can be quite painful. But hang in there, it will pass quickly."

Boy, was that an understatement. I closed my eyes and prepared for the worst. I thought. A few seconds later my head exploded, racking pain shook my whole body. I was being electrocuted!

Fortunately it did pass quickly. Though shaking uncontrollably and much weaker, I had weathered the storm. I opened my eyes to find both doctors watching me closely.

"You okay," the radiologist asked, as Dr. Morris held my hand and patted my shoulder.

Not so sure, I nodded yes.

"Very good. Brace yourself again. Only a few more dozen injections to go." The doctor was proving to be a man of few words.

Before I could respond, the medical implosion hit me again. I was no longer cold; I was in a cold sweat. The onslaught was relentless. I was losing my mind. They were removing my brain with an acetylene torch.

A few hits later I passed out. Thank God!

The Preacher

Pungent pleasures, atmospheres
Embalm the vapors of the mind
Dilute the sweetness of the hour
'Til fumes of void are all we find.

Consciousness came slowly, as I struggled for the light, somehow blocked by an object or cloud that seemed to hang closely over my face. My body was numb, and even attempts to turn my head were without result. I was totally paralyzed. My eyes worked but focus was difficult. It took a moment to realize what I was seeing. I was staring straight up, into the eyes of someone peering deeply into my own. Dark brown eyes with little or no white around them. The face too was brown, and the smell of the breath that mingled with my own was of nicotine, sweat and some kind of caustic medicine.

The voice was deep, guttural, almost a growl.

"If it wasn't for Jesus Christ, I'd just soon kill you right now."

I tried to speak, and then in a panic to cry out. But sound would not come. My throat was paralyzed too. I couldn't move, I couldn't cry out, I couldn't do a thing.

My observer leaned back, still above me, but out of my face for the moment at least.

Just when I thought he might spare me, the huge, dark man put a heavy hand on my throat. All I could do was watch, pleading with my eyes for mercy, praying in my heart for deliverance. The eyes looked confused, but the face calm, almost sympathetic, wavering between a smile and a scowl. In the dim light I could see the line of a wide scar crossing his forehead and encircling his scalp. It occurred to me that he must have had a lobotomy. Or might be insane.

I was helpless to defend myself and unable to call out. Long moments passed. He closed his eyes. The narrow bed swayed slightly as he began to rock back and forth, a low humming sound emitting from somewhere deep inside. His lips moved silently, mouthing what I hoped was a prayer.

Then, without a further sound he removed his hand from my throat and was gone.

Unable to turn my head, with limited peripheral vision, I could no longer see him. With the exception of a few moans, from various points around the room, all was quiet. Still unable to move, confused as to where I was or what was going on, I lay motionless for a long time waiting for him to return or someone to come to my aid. Sometime later I dozed back off.

The next time I awoke, how much later I'm not sure, I could turn my head. Looking to my left I found an empty bed. Beyond that was an old man, fast asleep, and beyond him it appeared there were quite a few other beds, some occupied, some not. To the right was the same. Though still heavily drugged, I decided I must be in a ward with a number of other male patients. I glanced back and forth. My previous visitor was nowhere in sight.

I noticed a nurse at the far end of the room, headed for the door. I tried to call out, but the words came low and slow. And then she was gone.

I stared at the ceiling feeling helpless and vulnerable. I had just closed my eyes when something bumped the bed. Fearfully opening them, my worst fears were realized. He was back. He looked at me and smiled, then turned to the bed on the left and picked up a pillow, turning toward me and holding it close to his chest.

I shook my head. No! This was it. After all we had gone through already, I wasn't going to need brain surgery after all. I was going to be smothered by someone who had already had his. I closed my eyes and prayed, waiting for the inevitable.

Nothing happened. I opened my eyes slightly, only to find he had turned away. He must have felt me watching, or heard me turn my head, for just as quickly he was back overhead. This time holding only the pillowcase.

He leaned down and grinned. A toothless, red-gummed grin that almost looked comical. "Jesus loves you," he said. Then he turned to the side, opened the drawer of the small table next to my head and began to load the contents into the pillowcase. I later learned this was where the medical supply kit they gave each patient was stored until needed. The last thing he pulled out was a pair of disposable slippers. He nodded and moved down to the next bed and table. I strained to watch while he was in my line of sight, and listen as he moved across and down the room. I heard a few protest from other patients but evidently most lay silently as he looted every bedside drawer in the room.

I caught a glimpse of him as he passed out the door, the bag across his back like a street person Santa Claus. It had been a long night. Just waiting and watching had worn me out. I scratched my nose without realizing it. The paralysis had passed, partially at least, and I knew that soon I would be back on my feet. I closed my eyes and prayed a silent prayer of thanks. "Thank you God, that Jesus loves me."

Sometime just after dawn a nurse came to my bedside with a pitcher of ice water. She helped me sit up and watched quietly as I surveyed the room. She grinned as I opened the drawer and showed her it was empty.

"Oh," she laughed, "Sorry about that. That was Old Charlie. He cleans out the place every night and hides his loot under his bed. He's been with us a long time. It's easier to put it back than keep him from doing it. He considers it his job. That and preaching a sermon to anyone that will listen each morning. Don't worry he's harmless."

"He may be harmless," I replied, "but he nearly scared me to death."

"Your wife is in the waiting room. As soon as you feel like it, you can get dressed so she can take you out of here. It's better if you go as soon as possible. And be sure to use the staff elevator and let the guard escort you to your car. That's a rough neighborhood out there."

Relaxing at last, I laughed with relief. "Looks like to me this is a pretty rough neighborhood in here too."

After getting me settled in, the officer escorted Pat around to the other side and closed the rental car door behind her. "Lock the door, and keep the windows up until you are on the freeway", he advised her. "Don't stop for anything; just get out of this area as soon as you can."

The gates with the razor wire slid open and we were on our way. Soon we were on the freeway, both sighing our relief. I was exhausted from the procedure and recovery. Pat was exhausted from the stress. And it soon became apparent; we were both just glad, for the moment at least to be alive. We agreed we'd worry about tomorrow when, and if, it got there. My head felt like it was going to explode.

We were almost to Pasadena before I regained my composure enough to tell Pat about my adventures of the night before. Before I had gone very far she interrupted me. "You mean Charlie?"

"Yeah, you should have seen that guy, he had scars…"

"I noticed. We had a good visit. He told me all about how he "got religion.""

"Are you kidding? That guy's a lunatic. I've never been so scared in my life." But somehow I wasn't surprised. Pat is one of those people others seem drawn to tell their life stories too. I don't know if it's her inviting smile or the endearing empathy so obvious in her eyes.

"I was frightened too when I first saw him." Pat continued. "He was wandering around the waiting room yesterday morning while you were having your procedure. At first he was just talking under his breath and quietly singing *JESUS LOVES ME.* Then he began waving his arms and shouting. That's when I realized he was preaching. Nobody was there, but he acted like he had a full congregation. He got so wound up his hospital gown came untied and his backside was hanging out. It was kind of gross and funny at the same time.

"I don't think he even noticed I was in the room until I got the coffee. Then the preaching stopped and he was right in my face. That guy was huge. I don't know what happened to him but he was in bad shape. Mentally and physically."

"Where'd you get that coffee," he demanded. Before I could reply, he leaned forward and sniffed the cup.

"I sure wish I had some," he said, "standing so close I started to get frightened."

"What did you do?" I asked her. For the moment, at least, I had forgotten about my headache.

"What do you think I did? I told him to take mine."

"What did he do?"

"He took it. Then, to my surprise, he said thank you, sat down in the chair beside me and started talking about his life and how he found Jesus."

"What happened to him?"

"I really don't know. He rambled on so I couldn't understand much of what he said. Mostly it was about how he loved Jesus and Jesus loved him. When the coffee was gone, he just got up and left, halfway through a sentence."

"Do you think he was crazy?"

"I don't know, but I sure was glad he was gone. And glad he loved Jesus."

Me too, I thought. About that time we pulled up to the Hilton Hotel. I had a few hours to clean up and get dressed before we headed for Huntington Memorial Hospital where my surgery was to take place early the next morning.

Halfway through my shower I realized I was humming *JESUS LOVES ME.*

Death and Rebirth

Clouds drift in, coming fast
Heaven's promise, near at last
But we hold on, grieve and pray
To live a lifetime every day
Too late we've learned, both what and how
To cherish life, here and now.

On October 9, 1975, I placed my fate totally in the hands of God. As the nurses rolled me toward the operating room, I told Pat I would see her on the other side, not knowing whether I meant the other side of the operation or the other side of heaven.

What should have been a seven-hour operation turned into a sixteen-hour marathon against death or total physical and mental devastation. On three occasions my heart stopped completely, and during the last hours of the operation my breathing was so shallow it had been impossible to monitor.

Less than an hour after it was over, I awoke and began responding to the doctor's questions. My vision was inverted, my heartbeat ran wild, and I felt exhausted, but I remember the instant I woke up as clearly as though it happened only this morning. For a moment I was confused. It was as if I had just returned from a long journey. There was something I was supposed to remember or do.

The tired and bloodshot eyes of the neurosurgeon, the one doctor in the world God had endowed with the ability and know-how to save my life were peering deeply into my own.

At first I thought I saw an angel, or maybe even God Himself, but then it dawned on me that I was still alive, and still on earth, in a wonderful hospital in downtown Pasadena, California. And it felt good to be alive! My joy was so great I felt like laughing out loud! We had won – God and I, and Pat, and all the thousands of other people who were praying for us.

"Raymond, Raymond," the doctor said, "Do you know where you are?"

"Downtown Pasadena," I quipped.

He turned to his nurse. "What? What did he say?"

Before she could answer he was on to the next question.

"Raymond, Raymond," he seemed to shout. "Do you know who I am?"

"You sure ain't no angel," I responded. This time he understood. Seeing first the surprise and then the broad smile on that great man's face, I knew everything was going to be all right. Then, no longer able to cope with the pain, I passed out.

When I next came to, the mounting pain was almost unbearable. A pulsating wave of unrelenting pressure, it stabbed without quarter at the base of my brain. But I was no stranger to pain. There had been surgeries and injuries before. Pain I knew could be endured. Pain would eventually pass.

But nothing had prepared me for the horror of that awakening.

Oh the terror! The fear, the disorientation, the sense of abandonment and betrayal. God was playing a cruel joke on me. I was falling into hell. My world was upside down and everything I confronted was out of kilter.

Floating in a fragmented kaleidoscope of grays and blacks, I was in every nightmare I had ever dreamed. Lost in otherwise endless darkness, violently erupting pinpricks of laser hot color bombarded my brain and burned away at what was left of my screaming soul. Searching for any way out, I arrived at a place that even in my state of confusion, I began to pray did not really exist.

Intermittently, I felt someone was near, waiting, watching, wondering when they would have a chance to take me away. I was weak, vulnerable, a shadow of the man I had been only a few hours before. I dare not move for fear I would fall. I looked up to see my feet. I looked down to see the ceiling. I was suffocating, smothered by the weight of my own body. It could only mean one thing. I had been crucified upside down.

A dark shadow offered me a drink. I gagged and tried to turn away. If I swallowed one drop, I knew I would drown. I clung to the surface above me, like a bat from the top of a cave. If I loosened my grip I would tumble to my death. My swollen head was throbbing, the blood draining down, crushing my brain. Each moment of consciousness became an eternity of submersion in a surreal dream. I tried to pass out again. Soon I was praying to die.

Then I heard voices. They, whoever they were, were teasing, tormenting me. I heard them talking. They said my head was up. They said it was the operation. They said it was the pressure of my brain swelling. They said I was out of my mind. But they offered me no help. Dark became darker until I heard or saw no more. I thought I was dead. And I was grateful.

Sometime later I woke up again. This time I knew where I was and remembered about the surgery. I also had vague memories that sometime in the night I had seen Pat's beautiful face and felt her caress on my arm. My parents had been there too, but I didn't remember when or for how long.

Still upside down, feeling like I was hanging from the ceiling, I held on tight. The vertigo was still there but the fear had lessened. I looked about, trying to focus my eyes. Someone had put goggles on my face. I peered about the room like a skydiver searching for a safe place to land.

On either side, hanging up from the floor, were thick curtains, a subtle line of light lining their upper ends. My architectural perception must have been sound, for I realized the space was not square. It was a truncated shape with the narrow point toward my feet. Below me, and behind my head, must have been the medical monitors, for I could hear the beeps and see a faint glow on the curtains on either side of my head. Near the floor across the pie shaped trapezoid at the narrow end of the curtains was a clock. And above that an opening in the curtains through which I could see a nurse sitting upside down at a desk hanging from the ceiling. At least I wasn't alone in my misery.

The vertigo was making me nauseous. I closed my eyes and tried to concentrate. The pain was starting to intensify, so I knew I didn't have long before I would black out again. I heard someone ask the nurse if it was midnight yet.

Eureka! They were wrong. Confused maybe, but no brain damage.

I opened my eyes and looked at the clock. It was still upside down, the twelve on the bottom. But it was reversed too. The three was on the counterclockwise side of the twelve!

About that time Dr. Morris came in. He must have seen I was awake and excited because instead of just checking me out he leaned over and spoke to me. Later he told me how the conversation went.

"How we doing?" he asked. "Still nauseated?"

"Yep, still upside down too." I whispered.

"Oh?"

"But now I know why."

"Oh, why?"

"My vision's inverted."

"Your inner ear gyroscope is messed up. That sometimes happens."

"I don't know if I can stand it for long."

He patted me softly on the shoulder. "Don't worry; everyone's vision is inverted when it first enters the eye. Your brain will correct it in a while."

"You look ridiculous hanging upside dow..."

I never finished the sentence, he told me. It was to become a recurrent pattern. Wake up from the pain, be alert for a while, and then pass out from the pain. Over and over again until I thought I couldn't stand it.

Sometime before daylight during that first night, I screamed out in agony, fully convinced I couldn't stand the pain for another hour. When the nurse came, I didn't ask her, I told her, "Find Dr. Morris, I want this to end. Now!"

Later, less than an hour I know because I had not yet blacked out again, he was there by my side, his reassuring hand on my shoulder.

"Dr. Morris, the pain, the pain is too much. I can't stand it. I'm not going to make it another hour. Do something now, make it end," I begged.

I remember hearing the nurse say something about a shot.

"Not yet," the doctor said, "it's too soon, his brain's still swelling. Maybe in a few hours."

"Doctor Morris, please!"

"Raymond. Listen to me. It's too dangerous for you to have any more drugs. But you can handle this. Focus on the clock. If you can't stand it for another hour, then stand it for ten minutes. And then stand it for another ten minutes until you pass out again. And then when you wake up, start all over again. Before long, the swelling in your head will go down, your body will begin to mend, and you'll be on your way to recovery."

Somehow through the fog, I heard him. And understood. I don't remember his leaving my bedside, only the snail-like movement of the second hand on the clock. For the next few days that clock was my lifeline to sanity and survival.

Knowing how critical the next few hours would be, Dr. Morris and his staff tried to keep me conscious and talking for as long as possible. I later learned it was to measure whether I had brain damage and to keep me alert and fighting for my life. Each time I woke up, they said, I rambled on and on until the pain became too much for me to speak. Sometimes I referred to my family, or life before the tumor. But most of the time it was about something they couldn't understand. On the threshold of death, my speech garbled, all I wanted to talk about was the "Light."

At first, they thought I was referring to a glow from one of the many monitors attached to my head and heart, or perhaps from a light somewhere outside the small triangular section of my curtained patient space that opened onto the central nurse's station.

Not until Dr. Morris brought in a psychologist to further evaluate the impact the swelling was having on my brain did someone hear me clearly enough to realize I was speaking not about the operation or my current situation, but about something very unusual that had occurred during the operation.

Over the next several hours, they later told me, I spoke often of having an out of the body experience similar to that of other patients who had had a life interruption and returned to tell about it.

Unknown to me, the book *Life After Death* had recently been published and there was a great deal of interest in the subject by professionals and students associated with both psychiatry and religion. During the period I was in intensive care a number of people, none of whom I later could name or remember, appeared by my bedside with notebooks and tape recorders in hand. At Dr. Morris's encouragement, I tried to explain what I had experienced.

By the questions they asked it appeared some believed at least some of what I said, and others believed little or none of it at all. At the time it really didn't matter whether they understood or believed, for I knew the truth, and even in my damaged state, I knew I knew. Exhausted and frustrated, I soon gave up on trying to explain.

At that critical time it was all I could do to talk, much less explain to anyone what I was talking about. Especially about something of such significance that it would change my whole comprehension of life and eternity.

After that first night, there was little or no time to think about what happened to me during that life changing operation. It was all I could do to hold on, cope with the pain, and convince myself that I wanted to go on living. For reasons I didn't understand for a long time, it would be many years before I would openly discuss the subject again with anyone other than my wife and children.

But one thing was sure. Life as I knew it no longer existed. My life, and my eternal destiny, were changed forever.

The Presence of God

As water seeks the lowest level
When springtime thaw brings forth the flood
And tears like drops fall downward ever
The soul of man for full completeness
Seeks undauntless for peace unsevered.

Immediately following the operation, Dr. Morris sought out Pat in the waiting lounge and tried to explain why the operation had taken so long. Although he was used to operating on patients with little or no hope, and it looked like I would survive, he nevertheless seemed surprised at the outcome. The tumor, he told her, had been pressing heavily on my life-monitoring brain stem. It was a situation so delicate even his skill and sophisticated equipment were not enough. Each time he tried to work in that area, my heart would stop. And he too would stop, trying to decide whether to give up or go on at the risk of my immediate death. On the first occurrence, when my heart started back up, he knew he must continue to try. On the second occasion, he had already been working four hours longer than the operation should normally last, and he decided he could go on no longer, that it was no use.

Once the heartbeat was restored, he ordered his assistants to close up. But as he turned to walk away, he said he felt a surge of new strength, new courage, as if some power outside himself had willed that he go on.

An hour and a half later, when the heart stopped again, he merely paused until the heartbeat again showed on the monitor, and continued with renewed strength, fully confident that it was God's will that the operation be a success. "You should have died," he later told me. "It's a miracle that you are here."

Over the next few weeks each member of that seasoned surgical team testified to Pat and me that they felt the very presence of God in that room that October day, and that never in their entire association with the neurosurgeon had they seen him perform with such strength and precision. Each of them had wanted to quit, to collapse from the strain, at one point or another, and each of them had experienced a resurgence of courage and strength and an infusion of the power of God that caused them to perform above and beyond their normal capabilities.

Several days later, after the most critical period had passed, I realized it would take as much courage to go on living as it had to face the threat of death. I could hardly talk. My vision was inverted. With no inner ear balance, I was incapable of standing erect. With the loss of the seventh nerve, the left side of my face was totally collapsed, without feeling and incapable of moving. My left eye, without tears, wouldn't even close. Without the application of artificial tears on an hourly basis, the vision on that side would soon be beyond recovery.

But worst of all was the psychological impact of losing my physical identity. Not only did I feel ugly; I couldn't even kiss my wife or smile at my children should I ever see them again. My ego shattered, and my strength sapped, I began to wonder whether death might not have been the greater blessing. The frustrations that followed the operation sometimes seemed to be greater threats to my wellbeing than the operation itself. Pain and frustration were destroying my will to live.

Fortunately I was not alone. God was with me, and so was Pat. In the days that followed she became God's physician as she patiently and lovingly stayed by my side, giving me the courage and the encouragement to learn to walk again, to swallow without choking, to talk again without drooling, and all the other simple tasks of life we take for granted. Throughout that ordeal, her smile and love were always there. But she was suffering too. The pain in her eyes reflected the pain in my battered body and soul.

It was only through the Grace of God and the miracle of modern medicine, also a gift from God, that I had survived. The power of prayer, my Christian upbringing and the example of my parents, my teachers, my friends, and the rest of God's earthbound angels that nurtured and cared for us made it possible for me and my family to survive the medical ordeal, the painful recovery, and the psychological trauma that followed. It took as much courage and Christian support to go on living as it had to face the threat of death.

Fortunately, we didn't have to do it alone. Even before I was out of Intensive Care, the phone in the hospital began to ring. Long distant calls came in by the dozens from little towns in Texas with names the nurses had never heard of. Places like Lake Jackson, Clute, Freeport, Angleton, Brazoria and Denton, Texas. And big cities too, like Houston, and Dallas, and Baton Rouge, and Shreveport, Louisiana. And even a call from Washington, D.C. Flowers and notes began to arrive, with special prayers and well wishes attached, from all of these places, and many more besides. We didn't have the Internet then, but it soon became obvious that throughout the nation and throughout the world people were praying to God on our behalf.

Two men I had never met, who lived in Pasadena, California where the hospital was located, came by on a regular basis to check on me. The nurses said they worked for Dow Chemical Company, the major employer in our hometown. Their fellow executives had told them that a lonely couple from Lake Jackson needed their companionship and support. When they saw how great was our need, their wives began to come too. Even the doctor, our world famous neurosurgeon who had been God's instrument in saving my life, came to visit on his off-hours. We became fast friends, each searching for additional strength.

You can imagine the difference it made to Pat, standing by helplessly, more alone than I could ever be, watching the man she loved being tortured to the threshold of death, and all the time living in a strange hotel, in a distant city, two thousand miles from our home and children. But it was a while before I was aware of the impact these caring Christians had, for I was out of it most of the time, just struggling to physically and psychologically survive. Earthly concerns, following the heavenly journey I had experienced, were far from my thoughts at the time.

The Journey

As I reached to embrace that heavenly glow
And the veil of life at last was rent
I no longer heard the eternal shout
Of loved ones lost and time unspent
But a voice of love in angels' song
"Come hither mortal lot.
Come smell the roses yet unborn
And share the hour of time that's not."

From the moment I awoke from that excruciating operation every aspect of my life has been influenced by an incredible spiritual experience that I have, until recently, always been reluctant to openly share. Neither because I am selfish or uncertain as to what did occur, nor because I fear doubt by others, but primarily because I am so sure that what I experienced was real. It is a core element of my belief in God and the afterlife.

I have always been a storyteller. A person who likes to spin a yarn, to reveal a truth by parable, or creatively relate an event. Like most "great" bards, I have often had a tendency to exaggerate a point or embellish the details to make the story more interesting. That's fine for entertainment and it's the stuff of which legends and myths are made. But it's not something I want to do with the most important revelation in my life.

At the height of that first operation, this is what happened, what I know and believe to be true.

Sometime during the period between the first and third time my heart stopped, I realized I was watching my own operation from somewhere outside myself. I could see my mostly nude body in a sitting position, back bent, arched face down across a table or frame. A number of people were gathered around so it was difficult to see, but I seemed to understand exactly every detail of what was going on. My laid open head was fixed in position by braces secured to each side. The surgeon, peering through a huge instrument, was working on the left side of my head.

I watched for a long time, intrigued, but almost indifferent.

Suddenly there was a flurry of activity, a cacophony of urgent voices, and the doctor, head bowed, seemed to be backing away. Then there was nothing, only darkness.

I was alone, moving through a great void at incredible speed. At some point the darkness began to take form, not a vortex or a tunnel, but a narrow valley defined by constant motion on either side. A pinpoint of light still very far away softly highlighted subtly moving shadows. There was a great rushing sound. Not the wind, or bells, but angels' songs, or possibly the voices of the millennium, the spoken wisdom of all whom had gone before. The shadows, now human in profile, were moving closer, arms outstretched, welcoming me. All speaking at once, they were equally clear, telling me the answer to every question I had ever imagined. The past, the present and the future all melded into one. I understood everything. Not only where I was and what was happening but the answer, I believe, to every question ever asked by mankind.

Physical reality was changing too. I looked at my hands. My body, still recognizable in its earthly form, was gradually becoming translucent and bright. It all made sense. Approaching the Light, I was becoming one with the Light. The sense of wellbeing, of belonging, bought the greatest joy I have ever felt. And I knew, I knew even then, I was in Heaven and rapidly approaching the throne of God.

But my being there then must not have been in harmony with God's plan.

When the Light became bright enough to see individual faces, my journey came to an abrupt stop. At the edge of the shadows, I recognized someone I had once known and loved. My grandfather, Papa, radiant but real, hands outstretched, was beckoning me to his side. Whether he spoke, or I heard his thoughts, I'm not sure, but the message was clear. I had to go back. There were people who needed me. There were things I still needed to do.

The feeling of being in that place was so wonderful, so beautiful, so peaceful, so comforting and so right; I truly didn't want to leave. I didn't argue, but Papa knew as he always had, how I felt. Suddenly thoughts of Pat, my children, and all the others I had left behind, overwhelmed my heart. There was nothing to say. Papa was right. I had to go back. My earthly destiny was not yet fulfilled. People needed me and God still had a purpose for my life.

Just as quickly as it began the journey was over. The speed with which I approached the Light was nothing when compared to how fast I came back. Like the strike of a lightning bolt, I slammed back into my body.

The next thing I knew I was awake, responding to the doctor's questions. My journey into the afterlife, though real for that moment at least, seemed little more than the shadow of a dream. Only later, when my battle to survive had subsided, did the memories of what happened come flooding back.

There is a time to live and a time to die. Through the Grace of God, my time to die had been postponed. The memory of Papa's message was a driving force in my struggle to recover. "God," he had said, "still has a purpose for your life." Until that purpose was fulfilled, I soon came to realize, Heaven would have to wait.

Healing

So flit and flirt small flighty one
Pretend you care then kiss and run
Sip the nectar of my heart
Seduce my soul and then depart.

As usual Dr. Morris was right, when the swelling went down, the pain became manageable. Soon thereafter they moved me into a private intensive care room. Everything was still upside down, but at least there was a window and the room was square, so my architectural sensibilities weren't offended quite as much. There was also a TV, hanging from the floor like the clock had been. It didn't take me long to realize almost everyone on the TV was left-handed. And upside down.

One day I was lying there, watching who knows what, when a small sparrow flew into the window on the left side of my bed and almost knocked himself senseless, landing in a feathered heap. Startled by the noise, I turned that way and strained to see him clearly with my one good eye. The patch on my left eye, and the possibility that the nerve damage on that side might result in permanent loss of vision, was almost as unnerving as the inverted vision in the other eye.

The little bird recovered quickly, shook himself briskly, and went on about his business of feeding on the small bugs he found on the window pane. He was a perky fellow, oblivious to the fact that he was in a most precarious position, hanging upside down like that. He seemed to be watching me too, probably wondering why I was upside down. But, unlike me he didn't seem to mind.

He kept cocking his head to one side as he hopped and chirped, and pecked. It was several minutes before I notice that he was missing his mark as often as he was scoring.

With the patch on my left eye, and elevated to a half sitting position in the bed, I was having trouble turning and seeing him. Just when the frustration about my own problems were about to reach the screaming level, he finally hopped clearly into view.

It was then I realized he too had problems. He was blind on one side. A small but gaping hole in the side of his head revealed the eyeball was totally gone. That explained the crash landing. As I was later to learn, it is almost impossible to judge distance with monocular vision. It also explained why he was missing so many bugs.

Suddenly I found myself thinking about someone's problems other than my own. I marveled for a long time about his tenacity. He just wouldn't quit. Every time he failed to hit the target, he would try again. Finally, he must have been satisfied he had had enough. To my delight, he didn't immediately fly away. Instead, he turned toward me, cocked his head to one side, and began to chirp a cheerful song.

Although simple in context, it was the most beautiful bird song I had ever heard. Finally he stopped, turned about several times, and flew away, almost colliding into a tree trunk as he drifted out of my line of sight.

When my physical therapist came in a few minutes later, she noticed the tear running down my cheek on the side of my eye that still worked. "Are you all right, honey?"

"Yes," I said, "I'm better than I've been in a long time. I'm just ashamed of myself at the moment." She knew better than to pursue that discussion.

"You feel like trying to stand up again? If this is a bad time, I can come back later."

"No", I said, "Let's get on with it. I'll try harder this time."

She seemed surprised. Up to that point, I hadn't even really tried. I was convinced that with my inner ear balance gone, and my vision inverted, I would never walk again. All I had done in the previous sessions was collapse, complain about pain in my garbled speech, and whine about the nausea caused by the vertigo.

How could she know God had sent a feathered angel to cheer me on? If that little bird could survive in his crippled state, and do it while expressing the joy of being alive through his song, then I could too.

I never saw that little bird again, but I wish he could have seen me. Within a few days, I stood erect for a few seconds without my therapist balancing me. Soon I could stand alone for several minutes without falling.

A breakthrough came when my inverted vision corrected itself. That was a weird experience,

Awakened by the pain in my head and unable to read, there was little I could do to distract myself in the middle of the night except watch TV. Everything was upside down so what was on didn't really matter.

About three o'clock one morning I was watching some silly soap opera, wondering how the actors could make so much ado about what I at the time considered minor problems. Suddenly the picture on the tube began to vibrate, rotated clockwise ninety degrees, held for a second and popped back into an inverted position. I thought it was my imagination. A few minutes later it did the same thing again, but this time it rotated 180 degrees, settling in the upright position all images are supposed to stay.

This time I knew it was in my head, not on the TV. I was so excited I punched the call button for the nurse. In that unit, with everybody in such dire straits, the nurses didn't ask about the problem over the intercom, they came running.

"The TV," I blurted, expecting her to be excited too, "it turned right side up."

Confused, she looked at me like I was crazy. "Looks okay to me", she said. "Do you need anything?"

Wanting to explain, I looked back at the TV. It was upside down again, but the nurse obviously didn't see it that way. After she left, I continued to watch for a fairly long time, hoping the picture would turn over again. But it wasn't meant to be that night. I fought off the pain for as long as I could, but the nausea overwhelmed me again and I passed out.

When I woke up a few hours later, everything was right side up. Just as Dr. Morris had predicted, my vision had corrected itself.

From that point on I had a fighting chance. It wasn't long before I could crawl without falling over. Soon I could make it to the hall where balance bars lined both sides. With great effort I could pull myself up. The therapist was with me but she held back, seeing I was now determined to do it on my own.

When someone passed in the hall, whether doctor, nurse, or fellow patient, it was terribly humiliating if I was still on my knees. My pride became a motivator, and soon I was on my feet more often than not. From the outset of the therapy, and even during the assisted bathing sessions, I insisted that Pat not be present. Not only would it have frustrated me, it would hurt her too much to see me struggling that way.

But she was always nearby, in the waiting room down the hall or in my room when I needed her. Each day she reconfirmed her love and loyalty to me, encouraged and supported me, and bragged on my small accomplishments to me or anyone else who would listen. I know I couldn't have handled it, couldn't have made it back, if she hadn't been there when I needed her love most.

In many ways, learning to talk again, to drink and eat without drooling, to swallow without choking, to manage the headaches, and fight off the depression were as hard as learning to walk erect again. Most of the time I felt like a slobbering fool. I had counselors and psychiatrists` and plenty of professional advice, but the key to my psychological survival was Pat and her unerring faith in God, and me.

One of our favorite things near the end of that phase of my recovery was to go out into the courtyard that could be seen from my window. Pat would push the wheelchair and we would both enjoy the tropical landscaping and the California sunshine. It was the one place we could truly be alone. And the only place I could forget my problems for a moment and be fully grateful to be alive. Secretly, I hoped we would see that little bird so I could share another miracle with Pat. But we didn't. I guess God's purpose for him as related to me was fulfilled.

Soon after I was walking again, Dr. Morris, in his empathetic wisdom found a way to help two of his patients at once. He asked me if I would visit a patient who had been operated on a week after I had my surgery. I had met him briefly before we both went under the knife. He was a lawyer, so his whole career was dependent on him being able to talk and communicate on behalf of his clients. He lost the use of one side of his face too. But he had not fared so well in the recovery process. He had become so despondent he had curled up into a fetal position and had refused to do anything to help himself in the recovery. If things didn't change soon, Dr. Morris told me, he would probably die.

When I came into his room, and he heard my garbled voice, he opened his eyes for the first time in several days. Whether he was just curious as to the outcome of my surgery, or simply surprised to see I was alive and getting about, I'm not sure. But for some reason he responded to my presence favorably.

For almost an hour, we carried on a subdued, stilted conversation that both of us had to struggle to understand. We both hurt, and we both cried, but there was a bonding there that could only occur between two wounded and crippled individuals who had been through the same war. At some point I told him about the sparrow. God's feathered angel I called him. Somehow he heard and understood. Just before I left his room, he took my hand and feebly squeezed it, saying something about some day he would see me again.

It was the last time I saw him before I left the hospital. But the nurses later told me he had come out of the depression, started to eat again, and was soon on the way to his own recovery.

I sometimes think that visit was as important to me as it was to the lawyer. Dr. Morris knew what he was doing when he brought us together. By helping my fellow patient I helped myself. I had my first glimpse of renewed self-worth that day, my self esteem was boosted, and I was more grateful than ever for the healing I had experienced to that point. I also realized how great it felt to think about and do good for someone other than myself.

Near the end of my stay in that wonderful California hospital where my life began anew, it occurred to me that I had not yet directly said thank you to Dr. Morris. Not only had he saved my life, given me hope, and convinced me I could and should go on living, he had also become my friend. He was not only a great surgeon; he was also a truly wise and lovable man.

The Doctor was a man of the world. A celebrity in his own right, he also must have been quite the social icon, for few nights went by that he didn't show up at the side of my bed, often in a tuxedo and sometimes with a bottle of champagne. One night, after several repeated requests, he brought a glass for me too. He knew I would be awake, for I could only sleep a few hours before the pain from the weight of my head on the pillow would wake me up. He also knew full well what alcohol would do to my swollen brain. He tried to warn me but I wouldn't listen. So I joined him in a toast at two o'clock that morning. One sip and I was out of it, for a few moments at least, until my head exploded in a flash of painful insight. He taught me an important lesson that night. And the message was clear. Few things would ever be the same again.

Most nights he had a story to tell, of one movie starlet or another that he had just been wooing. Now and then a celebrity name I knew came up, but most of the time it was some aspiring young thing that considered him the celebrity, and a rich and connected one at that.

It was about a week before I was to move into the Hilton with Pat, where I was to stay for a while as an outpatient, not only for medical reasons but so I could gradually be reintroduced to the outside world. During that time, Dr. Morris and his associates would be keeping a close eye on us.

All evening long, I had been thinking of what I would say to this great man who had saved my life. I finally decided I would come right to the point the moment he arrived, before he launched into an account of his night's adventures. Of course, I wasn't even sure he would come, and if he did, and I was asleep, I might miss him. He had mentioned he was going out of the country for a few weeks before long.

I must have dozed off, for the next thing I knew, there he was, bigger than life, looking older than Methuselah but smiling from ear to ear. I got right to the point.

"Dr. Morris," I said, "There's something I've been wanting to tell you."

I paused for a moment trying to compose myself. This was an important and emotional moment.

Seeing his opening he cut me off. "I know, I know, but there's something I want to tell you first." He said in all seriousness. "Raymond, my good friend, you saved my life."

"But I…" Now I was really confused.

"No, I mean it. You got here just in time. If I had gone to Sweden and married that airhead Ms. Sweden, we would have been divorced by now and she would have all of my money. At least what's left after all the other divorces."

Then he laughed that deep and throaty laugh I had so come to look forward to each night. But there were tears in his eyes, and I could tell the thought of our parting was making it an emotional moment for him too. Somehow we had become co-dependents in our mutual struggle to understand exactly what had happened in that operating room on that miraculous day.

He, as God's instrument, had saved my life. And I, as he told me, my survival representing the greatest miracle he had witnessed in his entire career as a surgeon, had given him a new strength and courage to carry on in a very exhausting and stressful career.

I had known from the outset, from the first moment I laid eyes on him, that the doctor was no ordinary man. There was a sureness about him that belied doubt. But there was also sadness. A sadness of one separated from the world by the very strength that brought those in desperation to him.

We never discussed religion, and I'm not even sure whether he was a Christian, a Jew, or what, but I do know he was a man deeply humbled by the miracles he saw, and who often seemed awed by the success of his own efforts. And somehow, though he never spoke of it, I feel he had a great secret, a great loss somewhere in his own life that was the basis for the overpowering empathy so obvious in his personal concern for my physical and psychological well being.

He never spoke of it directly, but I could see it in his eyes. Not only did he realize just how close to death I had really come, but also that something special, very special, had occurred on that October day my life was changed forever. And perhaps, I sometimes think, his life was changed too.

A few days before I was dismissed from the hospital, Dr. Morris asked me if I wanted to try another experimental surgery that he thought might save my eye and tone up the muscles on the sagging side of my face. He would detach a nerve from the left side of my tongue and hook it up to the stub of nerve that controlled the tears and blinking of my left eye and controlled the muscles in my face. It was only a seven hour operation he said. A piece of cake, I thought, compared to what I had already been through.

I wanted to get on with it right then. But there was a problem. There was a surgical cut on the side of my neck that wouldn't fully heal. We would have to wait.

I moved into the hotel where Pat had been staying for much too long already. We both wanted to go home and see the kids, but we knew it would be hard to leave them again. So we decided to make the best of a tough situation. We were together again and had some time to ourselves.

The next few weeks were heaven on earth. We rested, we played, and we loved like we had never loved before. The hotel staff made every effort to accommodate our special needs. Everyone we met seemed anxious to help us. The people from Dow had us out to their homes for meals and continued visiting on a regular basis. A lady we knew only through a remote third party invited us to her home for a picnic and a day in the sun. Members of the doctor's surgical team visited us at the hotel and took us out on the town.

All this reintroduction to society was extremely important, for I had survived, but there were moments of depression when I was not sure I wanted to continue to live. As a man, I thought I was destroyed. It was a long time before I was fully convinced otherwise.

The longer we stayed in California, the greater my anxiety grew. The surgical wound just wouldn't heal. Fearing I might do something desperate if there wasn't some psychological relief soon, Pat expressed her concerns about my growing frustration to Dr. Morris. He told us to go on home. We could come back when healing from the first surgery was complete. Pat made plane reservations and we packed our bags.

It had been an unbelievable journey. We had seen the Pacific, I had traveled to heaven, seen the world upside down, and experienced hell on earth and through the Grace of God had survived. Enough was enough; it was time to go home for a while.

Homecoming

Flight delayed, waiting
Life on hold, debating
Time found, could be
Time lost, we'll see.

There is no place to hide on an airplane. Space is tight, distractions are few, and all on board, between takeoff and landing at least, are momentarily destined for a common, unalterable conclusion to the trip. Some travelers require more space than others. Some require more attention. And all cannot help but be aware of the uniqueness of their fellow passengers.

That first trip home was a lesson in humility. Out of the shelter of the hospital, the hotel, and the homes and haunts of known Christian supporters, the expressions and reactions that confronted me ran the gamut of human emotions. Fear, pity, impatience, curiosity, indifference, and even apparent hostility by some; then kindness, concern, compassion, sympathy and empathy by others. But all took notice of my physical condition, and all reacted visibly in a way that the message was painfully clear. The subject of their scrutiny was very, very different, if not downright scary or weird.

For the first time in my life, I began to understand the full impact of perceived discrimination, whether real or imagined, deliberate or circumstantial. And the helplessness one feels when the reasons for being singled out are beyond their choice or control.

I was big, ugly, and walked with a visible stagger. My head and neck were covered with scars and stitches. My head was shaven and swollen, with only a stubble of new grown hair. Half blind, I wore a black patch over my left eye. The left side of my face was totally collapsed, frozen in a perpetual frown. I was deaf in my left ear so I couldn't tell the source of sound, much less hear or understand most of what was being said. My speech was garbled, my temperament was testy. Often in pain, I was physically and mentally exhausted.

That was on the outside. On the inside I was the same me. At least I thought so at the time. I had the same feelings, intelligence, education, beliefs, memories, heritage, hopes and human needs I always possessed. I had the same need to belong, to communicate, and to be loved and understood. And I had the knowledge that God still had a purpose for me, regardless of what other people thought.

I was harmless. But to the world, and the people on that airplane, I must have appeared like a cornered, wounded animal. A potential threat to them and myself. When I approached, most individuals looked like they were ready to cut and run. Fear was particularly visible in the eyes of the children. And sometimes in the eyes of the flight attendants.

Once again, God's saving grace was manifested through the woman by my side. Talk about the beauty and the beast. Pat's winning smile, her knowing touch, and her visible support and encouragement were all that kept me from going berserk. Impatient and insecure, everyone and everything seemed to be moving in slow motion. It was purgatory all over again.

I also learned the true meaning of being handicapped that day. The simplest things can become very difficult when you are physically challenged in a way that makes your needs unique from those of the general populace. And those who have normal faculties, though many probably would care and would offer to help, are often totally unaware of the nature of the handicapped person's disadvantage.

It started out innocently enough. The stewardess handed out the plastic headsets needed to listen to the in-flight movie. They were sealed in plastic wrappings to prove they were unused and clean. In spite of my fumbling hands, which trembled uncontrollably much of the time, I managed to get the package open, plug the tubular end into the receptacle on the back of the seat in front of me, then spreading the earpieces apart, place one earphone in each ear.

The movie began, the dialogue and sound track I could hear was clear, but only part of it came through. Even in my confused state, it took only a moment to realize what was happening. It was a stereo headset, designed for people who had the use of both ears.

I wanted to enjoy that movie. I needed to see and hear that movie in a normal fashion. The frustration, though probably minor in a normal situation, was totally unnerving. Pat tried to calm me down. But I was in denial, fully determined to solve the problem.

But some good comes out of almost everything. That moment was probably the first time since the operation that my creative instincts began to reassert themselves. I was determined to solve the problem. In those days, long before airport security was so tight, you could carry a pocket knife without being considered a public threat. Before anyone noticed, I removed the headset, took out my knife, and cut the end piece off the left side, sharpened the end of the amputated tube, punched a hole in the right side tube just below the ear piece, inserted the left tube into the right, and "eureka!" I had a monocular headpiece. I stuck the earpiece into my right ear, and settled back to watch the show.

By then, Pat was looking around to see if anyone was noticing my weird behavior. Those closest, and at least one stewardess, were showing a great deal of interest. But they were kind, or maybe noticing I still held the open knife in my hand, said nothing, only continued to watch, all the while exchanging nervous glances with each other. Pat put on her most winning smile, shrugged her shoulders, and shook her head slightly to acknowledge their glances.

Everything went fine for about three minutes until the modified headpiece began to feel uncomfortable and I decided to improve the design. I overcut the tubes and the whole contraption fell apart in my hands. Seeing Pat had placed hers in the pocket behind the seat in front of her, I grabbed it before she could protest and started on a new prototype. By that time, those sitting around us and that one stewardess must have realized what I was trying to do. When the second model failed, they bought into the project and began to pass additional headsets to me for working material.

I didn't see much of the movie, but intrigued by the challenge of my project, I forgot my discomfort, focused on the creative challenge, and actually enjoyed the rest of the flight. As we were leaving the plane, many of those who had witnessed my antics, smiled as I passed, patted me on the back, or made an encouraging, understanding comment. The stewardess looked at the pile of scraps she would have to clean up, gave me a reassuring smile, and wished us well.

"God helps those that help themselves," Papa used to say. By focusing on a solution, rather than bemoaning the problem or feeling sorry for myself, I had won the support and understanding of those around me. When they first saw me, I was a weird and wanton species of the human race. When we departed, they understood I was much like them, a fellow passenger of flesh and feelings, heavily confronted with the challenges of a unique human condition, but doing the best that I could.

A delay in our departure from LAX meant we were about to miss the last late night commuter flight from Houston to the small private airport in our hometown. As soon as we were in the terminal where we were to board, Pat, seeing I was about to collapse, helped me to the nearest seat, advised me to stay put, and raced off down the concourse toward the ticket counter on the far side of the terminal where our boarding passes were being held. The plane was already boarding. I was out of it, only vaguely aware we might not make it home that night. Though only fifty miles away, home might as well have been a million miles away if we missed that flight.

I was sitting there, alone and feeling abandoned, as the last of the boarding passengers vanished through the door that led to the loading ramp. Pat was yet to be seen down the long concourse where she had disappeared a few minutes before. It looked like all was lost. We'd be spending another night away from home.

Out of the corner of my eye I saw someone coming toward me. It was the well dressed middle aged man I had noticed earlier as the last passenger in the boarding line. He seemed in no hurry. I wondered if he was going to miss the plane too.

"You headed for Lake Jackson?" he asked.

"Yes sir," I said with some effort, "When my wife gets back with the boarding passes. If it's not too late."

"You live in Lake Jackson?" he questioned.

I nodded. "Yeah, but we've been in California for a long time."

"Are you Raymond Burroughs?"

Yes Sir," I said surprised. I was sure I had never met him before.

"We're holding the plane until your wife gets back," he said with a ring of authority. "Glad you're home son. We've all been praying for you."

I turned to look for Pat. When I turned back, he was gone.

We made it to the plane and were soon on our way. A small commuter plane, it held only about twenty passengers. I tried to spot the man who had helped us, but in the dim light I never could. It was several weeks before Pat told me he was a vice president of the Dow Chemical Company, the major employer in our area, and that he too had been on the flight from California. I'm not sure whether he spoke to her before he approached me. But it doesn't really matter. As far as I'm concerned he was another of God's angels sent to help look out for us. He was probably the only one in the terminal that night that had the authority to hold that plane.

An hour later when we landed in Lake Jackson I was on the verge of passing out again. Pat helped me from my seat and guided me toward the small door to the top of the stepped ramp leading to the tarmac below. For reasons I cannot recall, I insisted she go down first. Just as someone behind said watch your head I conked mine soundly, took one dizzy step and fell all the way to the ground. Fortunately for me it was a soft landing. Unfortunately for the two of the ground crew who had been alerted to help me when I got down, I landed heavily in their arms. Somehow they checked my fall before I hit the ground.

As I struggled to regain my balance, one of them asked me if I was all right.

"Yeah, I think so," I replied, "Just a little dizzy."

The other followed with another question. "Did you crash, or were you shot down?" he asked with mock seriousness.

Seeing his smile, I managed to laugh. Something I hadn't been doing much of since the day we left home. It hurt my face, but it still felt good. Maybe there was hope if I could laugh at myself.

But the adventures of the night were not yet over. Seeing I was about to collapse, Pat parked me on a bench just outside the door of the small terminal and told me to watch for our ride. She had made arrangements for her mother and Ramona to meet us at the airport. Robert, she had warned me, wouldn't be with them. He was in Beaumont with my older brother. Telling me to stay put, she went back inside to check on our bags.

The car pulled up a few minutes later. A neighbor was driving. I could see Ines in the front passenger seat, but I couldn't see Ramona. They stopped on the parking lot just a dozen yards away and turned off the lights. Torn between waiting for Pat, and going to the car, I waited for them to get out and come over.

Nothing happened. Anxious to hold my daughter again, I headed for the car. I saw Ramona in the back seat and reached to open the door. Instead of the excited embrace I so longed for, and the smiling welcome I so needed, her reaction totally unnerved me. Her panic was instant and unmistakable. Instead of sliding forward to meet my offered embrace, she scrambled away as far and fast as she could in the tight confines of the car. Her back up against the opposite door, she cringed down in terror.

At first, I didn't understand what had frightened her so. It took a few heartbreaking moments to realize she was fleeing from me. She had no idea who I was or what was wrong with the strange man who had tried to get in the car with her. Shaking from exhaustion, tears running down one side of my distorted face, my slurred words and frantic efforts to calm her only made matters worse. I watched in horror as the door she was leaning on swung slowly open. I thought she might fall. Or run away

Once again Pat came to the rescue. Coming out of the terminal just as I approached the car, she realized at once another painful crisis was in the making. Rushing to the opposite side of the car, she opened the door and wrapped her first born in a protective and comforting embrace, motioning me back at the same time.

Even in the reassuring warmth of her mother's words and embrace, it took several minutes to calm Ramona down. When I tried to approach her again she was still unsure. As we drove toward home, she buried her face in Pat's shoulder, still too confused and in shock to look at me. Not until we were safely home did I finally get that first hug.

A few days later, when my brother brought Robert home, I thought it through before I went charging out to greet him. Just outside the front door, I kneeled on the sidewalk and reached out both arms, offering a welcoming and waiting embrace. The car door opened, Robert jumped out, and calling out "Daddy!" came running toward me. About ten feet away he stopped in his tracks, looked about with a confused and scared look on his face, and started backing up.

Maybe in the daylight, I didn't look so bad. It only took about a minute of coaxing to get him to come to me. Seeing Ramona give me a hug did the trick. Soon thereafter I had them both in my arms. Only then did I feel I was truly home. Soon the love was there again, they began to understand what had happened, and the healing of our family was underway.

The days that followed were nerve racking. The wound on my neck just wouldn't completely heal. Every few hours, day and night, I had to put artificial tears in my left eye to keep it from drying up and self destructing. Four times a day, I had to shock my face, using a devilish device the doctor had prescribed that caused the muscles to contract in a painful way. The purpose of that miniature "cattle prod" was to keep the muscles from atrophying so the experimental surgery yet to come would have a semblance of muscle tone to work with that would allow the nerve graft to have some positive effect in restoring some balance to my face.

"You won't be able to smile," the doctor had said, "but at least your frown won't be so severe." It didn't promise much in that area, but it was all the hope I had to save my eye. I tortured myself relentlessly with that machine. At least it was something I could do for myself.

I hardly ever stepped out of the house. When visitors came, and many caring people did come, I made my excuses and left them to Pat. Night and day began to blend into one. I would sleep a few hours and then wake up from the pain; then be awake for a few hours before passing out from the pain. It was a vicious cycle I thought would never end.

Then suddenly, following a call to Dr. Morris, it was time to go back to California.

I remember little or nothing about that trip, only that I wanted to get through with the surgery so we could go home for good. Only seven hours long and without the brain involved, the pain and the misery proved minimal.

Once again, Dr. Morris's medical genius resulted in a successful experimental surgery. Although I would still have to use the eye drops and the shocker for a good while, I no longer was in danger of losing my eye. From that point on, every time something touched the point of my half collapsed tongue my left eye would close, tears would flow, and the muscles on the left side of my face would flex just enough to keep them in tone.

We returned to Lake Jackson, and the people opened their hearts and arms to us. Within weeks I was in business for myself, within a year we bought a nice home for our family, and for the first time in my life I found doing for others brought as much joy as doing for myself. Before long we were back in the mainstream of our community, and everywhere was the presence of God, and miracles for seeing on a daily basis. And it became obvious that the more we asked of God, the more he responded, and the more we gave, the more we received.

A New Start

I pray the years that still remain
Will be so full that I will gain
Insights lost in years gone by
So I might live before I die.

Even though many people helped us during those early weeks of readjustment to life, there was one individual who was proving very difficult to deal with on a day to day basis. He thought I was ugly, couldn't seem to cope with the idea that my life was changed forever, and expected me to continue as before with little or no compassion, empathy, or sympathy.

Each morning he seemed uglier and angrier than ever. There was no escaping the inevitable, no way of avoiding the daily confrontation. Every time he looked at me he saw the same thing; an ugly, contorted face, a near-death mask that destroyed all hope for finding or expressing joy in being alive. All I had to do to meet the enemy was look in the mirror. What I saw there was not a nightmare, not some fictional beast that would disappear when I woke up, it was me.

In the depths of self-pity, I momentarily forgot the miracles, God's many blessings, and the support and prayers of those who loved and cared for me. My promise to God, seeing the Light, and the message from Papa during my short sojourn in heaven, all seemed distant memories clouded by the fog of current reality. As the burden of despair became heavier and heavier, pressing and depressing, there was a short period there when I began to seriously question whether or not life was worth continuing at all, and that everyone, including myself would be better off if I was no longer around.

Seriously considering suicide, trapped in an endless cycle of self reinforcing mental hell, I forgot what Papa told me as a child. *If it was good enough for God, it ought to be good enough for me.*

Just when it appeared all hope was lost, Pat once again came to the rescue. The song *"The Way We Were"* was a major hit at the time. Every time I heard it I would have an emotional breakdown. One day as that heart rendering song was playing on the radio, seeing I was about to loose control again, Pat asked me a simple question that made it possible for me to cope with the reality that life would never be the same again. "Raymond," she said, her own pain evident in her voice, "was it really all that good before?"

The question went unanswered but I suddenly came to grips with the fact that I, through the grace of God, and only through the grace of God, was still here on earth. If I was willing, I realized, life could be better than it had ever been before. God would help and the miracles would continue. But it was up to me to overcome the physical and psychological barriers that threatened to hold me back.

It was a critical turning point. From that moment on my thoughts were not about what was bad about life, but what was good, and what I could do to make it even better. Not just for me, but for my wife, my family, my friends, and all of God's children who share and participate in this journey we call life. And I decided it was high time I quit waiting for help from others and started being part of the solution myself. Once again I remembered that God helps those who help themselves.

The question was what to do. I was a mental and physical mess, no longer employable as a major player in an established business. I had no financial capital, little strength or endurance, and practically no patience with myself or anyone else. I wasn't very attractive either. In fact, I was downright scary to anyone who didn't understand what was going on in my life. Without a smile, unable to speak clearly, wearing a black patch over my damaged eye, and often struggling to stay conscious and keep my balance, it appeared I had few choices. Hire out as a freak in a circus sideshow, become a drunken pirate, or maybe.....

That was it! I could go back to doing what I had been educated to do using the God given talents I had been wasting while I chased the almighty dollar. I had been a good architect before and I could be one again given enough time and the right opportunities.

The next day I delivered an article announcing the opening of my architectural practice to the local newspaper. The article spoke of my education, experience, and awards I had won in my former days. The picture looked just like me; before the operation. It gave my home phone number but it didn't say I would be working off my kitchen table. It didn't say I could only work a few hours at a time before the pain put me out of commission. It didn't say I was desperate to be the old me again. It didn't say I had no where else to turn or that I had a wife, two children and a mother-in-law who were counting on me to put food on the table.

Since we had returned from California, Pat almost never left me alone by myself, at home or anywhere else. But a few days after the news release, for reasons I cannot remember, she did just that and for the first time I remember everyone was out when the doorbell rang. I was so self conscious about my appearance I almost didn't go to the door. But something told me I should.

The gentleman at the door was almost as frightening as me. I remembered his face and long beard, but not his name, for I had I never had an opportunity to pay attention to him up close. Short and stout, almost ferocious, with a longshoreman's demeanor, I had seen him at numerous city council meetings during my former days as vice-president of the home building company. He was one of those guys that is a self appointed conscience of all bureaucrats and elected officials. A union man in an open shop community, often unpopular, but often right, he was the public watchdog for the "little guys" in our community.

Before I could speak he boomed, "Are you Burroughs, the architect?" He barged in the door before I could even respond. He pulled out a sketch of a home site on the corner of one of our local streets.

"Now here's what I need. With my grandson starting to drive, what we need is a third garage on the house where my son lives. I like to have something to present to the planning commission week after next. The pay is five-hundred-dollars or whatever you think its worth. Payable on delivery."

"Well, Yes Sir," I stuttered, looking at the sketch. The only place to add another garage onto the house was over the driveway. "But the codes won't allow a tandem garage. The city manager would never..."

"Don't you worry about that old coot," he continued, "I've got a little pull myself."

I knew from experience, that "old coot" wasn't going to be influenced by anyone or anything but what the city code required.

"But..." I stammered

"No butts! You handle the design and I'll handle the politics," he said with finality, "Give me something to sign as a contract and call me when it's done."

I wrote up a one paragraph contract, and put Three-hundred-dollars for the fee.

"Don't you hear good son? I said five-hundred-dollars." He scratched through my number, put in his, and signed the paper.

Before I could comment further, he was closing the front door behind him.

Pat had mentioned the rent payment was due, so I asked her to take me to the bank as soon as she got home. Man was I in for a dose of reality that day. The bank where we had kept our money before we lost it all wouldn't give me a loan even though I had a signed contract as collateral. The story was the same at the next one I tried. Finally, at a third bank I had never used, I met a lending officer who had seen hardship himself. He had an ongoing disease that had hindered his career from the outset. He had empathy. He made me a loan equal to one hundred percent of the contract amount.

My family and I had steaks that night. I felt a slight glow of positive self-esteem returning. It tasted as good as the steak.

It didn't take long, but drafting up that site plan took longer than it should have. I couldn't see, my hands shook, and my neck and back hurt most of the time I was working, but somehow I got that first job done.

The following weekend I gave my client a call. He came right over, nodded his approval, and gave me a check for five-hundred-dollars. He must have been pleased, he was whistling as he walked out the door.

The following Monday, I went to my new bank and paid off the loan. I had a new contract too. A friend of mine wanted to remodel an old grocery store into an office building. My fee would be One-thousand-dollars and six months free rent if I would office there.

The banker asked if I wanted another loan. I said yes, but for Seven-hundred-and-fifty-dollars. This time I would make a profit. My architectural career was underway. There have been many projects and many loans since; and some profit.

I kept watching the paper for some mention of my first client's project, but nothing ever appeared. It was a while before

I realized my suspicions were true. He never really intended to pursue that project. I had earned my fee but the opportunity to do so was pure charity. The town conscious, like so many of God's angels, had empathy for those he felt were less fortunate.

The House That God Built

Of all the things that waste away
One cannot buy an extra day
Though the end of time now seems like never
A day that's gone is gone forever.

About a year after I started my business and our lives as a part of our community seemed fully underway again, I came home to find my oldest child terribly upset. She was unusually withdrawn, turning her face away when I tried to find out what was wrong. Pat explained to me later the other children at school had been teasing her.

"She feels insecure," Pat said. "I think some people in town think we aren't going to survive the aftermath of this thing. Children sense these things, hear their parents talk, and repeat what they've heard. We've got to do something to prove to our children and this community we're here to stay."

Only then did I realize that though I was managing to cope with what had happened and the physical impact of my disfigurement, it wasn't so easy for those who had to live with me and claim me as their own. Evidently, it was especially difficult for my children, at home, in school or at play with their peers.

"Honey, I'm working as hard as I can. Business is good, and folks are beginning to realize that I'm better at designing buildings than I am at smiling. They don't care what I look like once they understand what happened." I rationalized.

"It's not the ones that understand. It's the ones that don't understand." she continued, "Or know. But, it's not them I'm concerned about. It's us. And the kids."

"What can I do? It doesn't look like my smile is going to get any better any time soon. We'll just have to hold on until things get better."

"I've got a better idea. We can prove to ourselves and the world that we're here to stay." She smiled.

"Just how are we going to do that?" I questioned.

"Remember that house we were going to build before the surgery?"

"Well sure, but then we were financially flush and I was vice-president of a major home building company. It's all I can do to meet payroll now."

"We need to live in a home that you designed to prove to ourselves and the community that we are here for the long term."

"I don't know Pat. It takes money, it take time, and it take's energy. I don't know if I'm up to it."

"That's just the point. If you don't believe in yourself, how can you expect anyone else too? We need to do this Raymond. If not for ourselves, for the children. You can do it. We can do it. With God's help, we'll find a way." She concluded.

When someone believes in you like that, how can you refuse to try?

So we built the house that we live in as I am writing this book of miracles. And there are reasons that we don't move on. It's more than a house. It's our home that God built.

Not long after that discussion took place, two young men fresh out of a northern college dropped by the office seeking work. Both had graduated with degrees in construction technology. One of them had grown up around construction, his father did residential remodeling, but neither had much practical experience. Both seemed confident they could do anything they set their minds too, if only someone would back them in the construction business.

It was a win-win opportunity. They didn't want much pay, just an opportunity to get started. I didn't have much to pay; I just wanted to build that house for the family.

I thought and prayed about it for a few days and decided to take yes for an answer. Once more, it seemed, God was showing me the way. "Here's the deal", I told them. "I'll start a construction company, buy the tools and a truck, and find a way to finance our projects. We'll try remodeling for six month's or so, and then if things work out, we'll take on my house. When it's finished, I'll sign over the company, the tools and the truck to the two of you and you'll be in business for yourselves."

"Are you serious?" one of them asked. "What's the catch?"

"No catch," I said, "You need jobs and an opportunity to get in business for yourselves, and I need someone to build my house." I pulled out the house plan I had been working on to see how they would react. Huge and custom, it was not like any house they had seen before. They didn't even blink.

"When do we start?" they asked almost simultaneously.

"We start Monday." We agreed on hourly wages for the two of them and I asked them to come up with a list of basic tools they would need.

By the time they were in their old car outside, I was on the phone with a client of mine who had recently asked if I would consider designing and building the expansion of his home.

The next morning he called back. "My wife is really excited. We really got burned on that last remodeling. She said getting the construction done by someone she knows and trust is the answer to her prayers." It was the answer to my prayer too.

Soon there were other projects to work on. It didn't take long to prove our neophyte construction company was quite capable of handling anything that came along. At least in the residential remodeling field.

The guys worked hard, used their heads, planned carefully, and followed through on critical details. We didn't make money, but we learned a lot and their confidence grew. Soon I felt we were ready to take on a full house project.

Knowing what and how we would build, finding a site to build on was the next step. Figuring where wasn't hard. Pat and I wanted to build in the same neighborhood we had planned to build in before the tumor turned our world upside down.

How to pay for it was another matter. The chairman of the board of the savings and loan that was developing the next section of the subdivision where we wanted to build also liked to survey. He personally was staking out the lots the day I started my search. We knew each other well, because his savings and loan financed many of the houses for the home building company where I had been vice president. He, the president, and the vice president of his company were all good Christian businessmen well respected in our community.

The chairman was also known to be a tough negotiator. Trying to decide how to approach the subject of buying the lot, I watched him work several minutes before he noticed I was there.

"How you doing Raymond?" he asked with sincere interest, "I understand your architectural practice is getting off to a good start."

"Yes Sir, things are going well. Working hard and making a little bit of money."

"Just keep on keeping on. You'll make it okay. How are Pat and the kids?"

"Doing well." I said, "But hoping to do better. We're thinking about building a house."

"Sounds like a smart move to me. Where do you plan to build it?"

"Well, that's what I wanted to talk to you about. We'd like to build out here. In fact we'd like to build on that end lot by the park."

He looked surprised. The lot I was referring to was the largest in the subdivision, at the end of a street that dead-ended into a park, and backed up to a lake. He knew, and he knew I knew, it was probably the most expensive lot in the subdivision; the newest and most expensive subdivision in the area. I had figured there was no way we would get it, but I had promised Pat I would at least ask if it was available.

Probably to spare me the embarrassment of knowing I couldn't afford it, he offered me a way out. "Raymond, you know we only sell to builders. The lots go on sale Friday of next week. They'll be gone in an hour. If you want, I'll call you and tell you who got that lot."

"I'm a builder," I blurted out much too emphatically. "We started our company a few months ago. Right now, we're just doing remodeling, but our goal is to be full-scale home builders before the year is out. We've got two projects underway. I can give you some references if you need them. Folks you know."

He looked offended. I thought I had blown all chances of getting a shot at that lot. "Raymond, you know better than that. If you say you're a builder, then I have no doubt you are one. And probably a good one too." he added. "But you know from previously working with us, we have a six lot minimum. I don't know if the other guys will go along with selling just one lot to someone. It might seem unfair to the other builders."

With that I gave up; for the moment at least. He was right. I was in way over my head. I wasn't one of the big guys anymore. I was just another new businessman looking for a break.

But the good Lord must have had another plan. The following Monday, the chairman called me with good news. Sales started at nine on Friday morning. If I would show up at eight, I could have a shot at the lot of my choice.

Like a hunted rabbit in the field, I had jumped up. Now I had to figure out which way I was going to run. Time for more prayer. The silent conversation, the ongoing dialogue between me and my Maker that dominates my private thoughts, focused on one more request.

Friday morning, I was there fifteen minutes early. I had to wait for them to open the building. The chairman, the president, both elderly gentlemen, and the vice president, not much older than me, were all there.

They opened up a plat and showed me the layout. The end lot by the park was number seventeen, and sure enough, was the most expensive in the subdivision.

I put my finger on that one and said that's the one I wanted.

"Fair enough, but no surprise," the chairman said. "How do you want to pay for it?"

"I don't know. I don't have any money."

They looked at each other knowingly. They all knew my story. There are few secrets in a small town. "Raymond," the chairman asked kindly, "how do you expect us to sell you a lot if you don't have any money to pay for it?"

"Don't you let builders pay a deposit to hold their lots for a while?"

"Well, yes we do. We require a $500 dollar deposit to hold a lot for sixty days. Have you got $500?"

"No, sir, I don't."

The young vice-president spoke for the first time. "It's ten minutes till nine. We're running out of time."

I said a prayer under my breath, and made one last try to save the day.

"Don't you usually give a discount to builders?"

The chairman looked at me questionably. "Yes we do. We offer a $500 discount on the first lot."

"Then why don't we let that discount serve as my down payment," I asked feeling almost foolish.

There was a long silence as they exchanged thoughtful glances. Then just as the clock chimed nine o'clock, the chairman winked at the president and broke out laughing. Suddenly they were all laughing. I was just turning for the door when the chairman spoke up.

"Sold!" the chairman exclaimed. "But don't let anyone out there know how you pulled this off. We're supposed to be tough bankers. You've got sixty days."

They were still laughing as I left the office and a half dozen builders came clamoring in.

It's a start, I thought. Thank you Lord.

The next week, with knowledge I had a place to build, I would need to start looking for financing to pay off the lot and build the house. All weekend, all I could think about was a saying my Urban Law professor at Rice University came up with one day when we were talking about litigation.

"Sue for a million, hope for a thousand, pray for a hundred and settle for fifty," he offered as an explanation of how some lawyers work. Somehow fifty seemed like the right number. Not fifty dollars, but fifty percent of the cost of the house we planned to build.

On Monday I called the vice president of lending at a large savings and loan in Galveston. I had referred a great number of potential home buyers to him for home loans when I too was a vice president. But I knew it was a long shot. Bankers are in business to make money from loans, not foreclose on bad mortgages. Lending guidelines would be working against me.

He agreed to have lunch with me for old times' sake. He knew what had happened to me so it was a surprise when I brought up the request for the loan.

"How much do you need?" he asked cautiously.

"I want interim financing for fifty percent of the projected construction costs and a take-out commitment," I said.

"How much?" he repeated.

"Seventy-five thousand."

"How big is this house?" He looked surprise.

"With the lot, it'll probably appraise for one-hundred and fifty." I said, trying to look nonchalant.

"Where is the rest of the money coming from?" He questioned.

"I didn't say it would cost that much to build. I got my own construction company now. That should save some, and I can earn the rest through my architectural practice."

"Things must be going well." He thought for a minute and for some reason decided to take a chance.

"Okay, I'll run it by the loan committee. I'll need your financial statement, and last year's tax return."

"Might not help." I said, almost whispering.

"What do you mean, might not help?" suddenly sounding like a tough banker.

"I've got a negative net worth due to the surgery, and since I just started my architectural firm last year, I didn't exactly earn a lot of money."

"Then how do you expect me to present your request to the loan committee? All they care about is how you're going to pay back the loan. Don't you have anything I can offer as collateral?"

I remembered the lawyers quote. Time to sue for a million.

"I've got a lot to build on."

"You've got a lot?"

"Well, not exactly, I've got an option on a lot." I explained what had happened with his old friend the chairman the previous week.

"He did what? He tied up his best lot for sixty days on nothing more than a prayer."

Suddenly, he relaxed, shaking his head, a broad grin on his face.

"Okay, okay. I'll run it before the committee. It's a long shot, but I've seen that bunch make crazier decisions. But don't get your hopes up. I'll call you next week."

"Thank you sir," I said as we exchanged handshakes. And thank you Lord I silently prayed. Maybe, I thought, I should have asked for a hundred thousand.

Two weeks passed before I heard back from him. I figured he was reluctant to give me the bad news that our request had been denied.

"I told you they were crazy," he phoned to say on a Wednesday afternoon. "The committee said we could make the loan if you can find a 'straw boss' to sign for the interim." I thanked him profusely. I knew from experience, without his recommendation the proposal wouldn't have even been considered. Christian charity is where you find it.

Ines, Pat's mother, volunteered to be the "straw boss." Regulations at that time required a different entity borrow the construction financing. She really wasn't taking any of the risk, unless we didn't finish the construction and couldn't use the permanent mortgage commitment to pay off the interim financing. But it still took a great deal of faith for her to sign a note for such a large amount of money.

Within a few weeks we were underway. Most of the work was done by my two-man construction firm, with the help of a few day laborers now and then and an occasional subcontractor that required a license to do the work. I was amazed at how much my young builders knew, and equally amazed that when they didn't know they went to the library or did research to find out. They'd read about it one day and be out there doing it the next. Pat and I helped too, after hours on work days, sometimes under the lights, and on most weekends. Mainly doing cleanup and unloading lighter weight materials.

The biggest challenge for me was finding a way to come up with the balance of the construction costs. Every Friday I found myself struggling to meet payroll at the office, make payroll for the construction company, and to keep the overdue bills of material vendors to a minimum.

From the outset, I approached material suppliers, told them the truth about the nature of the venture, and asked for credit and longer than normal time to pay their invoices. To my surprise, all except one of the local merchants I approached agreed to do what they could to help. I later found out the individual I was talking to in that case actually didn't own the company he managed, so it truly wasn't his choice.

Small town interest paid off too. Once the house was framed up, folks we didn't even know would drop by and ask if they could have a tour. Extremely contemporary for it's time, the design, one of the best I've ever done in my opinion, looked much larger than it actually is, and contained quite a few innovations in the layout that are still unique to this day. A large volume space, accented with structural clarity, careful layered massing, and ample natural light, it opens up onto to the natural environment that stretches to the park and the lake behind. Sited to screen off neighboring houses, with none behind, it's more like a home in the country. But with full city amenities.

At some point the local newspaper picked up on what was going on, ran a few pictures and articles, and the number of visitor's and community support increased even more. Not one to miss an opportunity to publicize what I do for a living, I told a few of them we would be lifting the forty foot wood truss I had designed to clear span the second story library above the living room on the following weekend.

It turned into a barn lifting. A number of people showed up to watch the following Saturday, some with sack lunches and coolers full of drinks. Others, without, soon found they were welcome to the party and the goodies.

To lift the truss we had rented a large crane with a thirty-foot boom. When the lift started, I climbed on top and held onto the lifting cable for dear life, as the truss seesawed back and forth from the center balance point while it was lifted into place to settle into the upright end walls we had built to support it. Clearance was minimum, so I don't know what I would have done if the truss had proven to be too long or short. I probably would have leaped to my death rather than face the professional embarrassment of having missed the mark on my own project.

But it fit; I got down safely to a round of applause, and Pat finally forgave me for showing off at the risk of my life. She knew what the others didn't. Because of the surgery I had no inner ear balance, making me dependent on visual alignment to stay erect. Even now, if I loose sight of my cue points, or my vision is blocked, I can not stay vertical for longer than a few seconds.

After that weekend the roof went on, things calmed down a bit, and the slow struggle to finish the interior got underway. My architectural business continued to grow, the cash flow was good, and somehow we managed to meet our obligations. The Lord continued to show us the way and we were headed for the homestretch. It looked like another miracle was in the making and this time with minimum pain.

Then tragedy struck. One winter morning following a weekend Christmas social the night before, I came by, as I often did, to check out the previous day's progress. As I drove up, I noticed a two-by-four sticking through one of the front windows. Vandals had been at work. But not until I walked through the front door did I realize the magnitude of the damage. The first thing I noticed was how cold it was inside, and the steady breeze flowing across the living room. Then, the crashing of falling glass.

To my horror, every pane of the ten-foot high forty-foot wide glass wall across the back was broken out. Portions of safety glass, fragmented into millions of pieces still hung from some of the frames but not a single pane was left intact.

I almost fell as my foot skidded on a small ball bearing sized pellet. Someone had shot out every pane of glass, not just in the great room, but in every room in the house. I thought I would throw up. It was more than vandalism; it was an act of terror, a Mafia hit, or some other demonic act that sought to destroy our dream. How could it be? And why?

The front-page picture in the paper the next day told the community the story, sparing me the necessity to explain the unexplainable.

To this day we don't know who did it. The fact that the insurance covered only about ten-percent of the cost to recover was bad, but the gut wrenching reality of what had happened was even worse. From that point on, it was truly a struggle to finish.

But again, good Christian people came to our aid. Some lent a hand in the work, some extended credit, but most just gave us much needed moral support. And we almost made it to completion.

One of my two young contractors became so discouraged by the destruction that he decided to pull up and go back up north. That meant Pat and I had to step up to the plate and fill in the gap. One of the last large tasks was nailing in place the tongue and groove clear heart cedar siding that would cover the exterior, It was a beautiful, relatively light material that was fairly easy to install, but there was an awful lot of it.

On weekends Pat would hand us the boards and my remaining employee and I would position and nail them into place. A part of the work was from the ground, but an equal amount had to be done from scaffolds. It was a task so slow we couldn't realistically see the end of it before the interim loan, extended two times already, was due to be paid off. I began taking off from work at the office early a few days a week, but it still wasn't enough.

Then another miracle occurred. One day while the three of us were struggling to make progress, a man I didn't even know walked up and asked if we had another nail apron. He took a hammer he had brought with him and began helping with the siding. Before the day was out we were good friends. He worked for one of the larger companies in the area, lived down the street, and had been following the job from the day we broke ground. Before he left that day he promised he would be back the following weekend.

Thank you Lord!

The following weekend he was back. This time with several of his friends, all with their own tools. We really made some progress that weekend. There was still hope we would make our deadline.

The next weekend he and his friends were back, and a half dozen others too. By the end of that weekend, the siding was up. God's earthly angels are good carpenters.

Just a little more to go. A measure of completion that had been determined as sufficient to close on the permanent financing by the lender was installation of the final finish material, the carpet. Unfortunately I didn't have enough money left to pay for it, earned or from the loan. We needed more time.

I called my friend who had made the loan and asked him to extend the commitment one more time. He said he couldn't do it. The bank examiners were coming the following week, and they would classify the loan as a bad debt and cite the bank for a credit policy and regulation violation, and he would have to call the loan.

"What are we going to do?" Pat asked, her faith waning too.

"We're going to get that carpet, that's what we're going to do." I said, not sure whether I was trying to convince her or myself, "We've come too far to lose this thing now."

The next day I went to the carpet store. I already owed the owner an outstanding sum for the bathroom tile.

"How much deposit did you say you needed to order that carpet?" I said, fully expecting him to bring up the invoice for the tile. "I've got less than two weeks to get it installed."

"Doesn't matter what it cost," he replied, "it'll take six weeks to get it delivered. And another week to install it."

I thought for a minute, searching my brain for an answer.

"Can you order it, and then put a hold on it. When I come up with the deposit we can close on the order?" I blurted out, visibly excited.

"Yeah, I guess we could," he said, "But I thought you only had two weeks."

I walked over to where the installation materials were displayed. "Have you got enough of these tack strips in stock for the installation?"

"Sure, but they aren't much good without carpet," he laughed.

"How long would it take to put them down?" I asked.

"Probably a day or so. With two men working," he answered.

"Trust me one more time. Deliver all we need to the house and put them on my tab. We'll install them ourselves. And order and put on hold that carpet." I asked hopefully.

"Oh, what the heck. We're both going down the tube anyway. I'll do it tomorrow," he said with a grin.

With many thanks, I was on my way, trying to formulate the words to convince those bankers to close that loan. Lord, I prayed, this time I need more help than ever. This thing has gotten bigger than me.

I called my friend at the savings and loan that evening. "The carpet is ordered but it's on hold until I can come up with the deposit," I told him truthfully.

"You think we could go ahead and set up the closing."

"Can I honestly tell the examiners the job's substantially complete? What do I say if they ask about the carpet?" he asked

"Tell them it's in the process of being installed," I suggested.

"I thought you said it was on hold at the plant. How can it be in process of being installed?" he questioned.

"We're installing the tack strips tomorrow. That's part of the installation process." I exclaimed.

There was a long silence. "Well, I guess technically that is part of the installation process. Okay, I'm convinced. We'll set the closing for the middle of next week. Just don't come back to me for another loan," he added with a laugh. "And pray the examiners don't ask for on site verification."

Praise be to God. We were going to make it.

The loan closed, Ines was off the interim note, and we moved in on concrete floors. Keeping the kids off those needle sharp tack strips was a challenge, but somehow we survived until the carpet was installed. Otherwise, we were in architectural heaven.

It took a few months, but I managed to pay off all the vendors, settled up with my remaining construction partner, and we were in our dream home to stay. Soon the rest of our lives were underway.

Pat was right. If you believe in yourself, others will too. And some of them, especially God's angels here on earth, will buy into your dream and even help make it come true. Especially, if they believe you have God on your side.

Lessons

Sunlight, moonlight, stars at night
Wonders near, distant sights
Blue sky, hills, oceans deep
Smiles, tears and restful sleep.

A number of years after the surgery, my family and I were on our way back from a family Christmas gathering at my parent's home in Shreveport, Louisiana. It was a beautiful holiday spent with family and friends with the added aura of snow on the ground.

We were approaching Lufkin, Texas, when a huge truck overtook us and I changed lanes to let it pass. The young truck driver honked his horn and waved as he went racing by. My son commented on what a cheerful mood his smile conveyed.

Five minutes later we caught up with him. But this time the smile was gone. The eighteen-wheeler had jack-knifed on an icy exit ramp and overturned. The handsome young driver was dead.

As we drove on, silenced by the reality of what we had seen, I couldn't help but wonder what that young man was looking forward to that made him so cheerful when he passed us a lifetime before. I hope it was about his family and friends and a God filled Christmas.

On another trip when I was returning to Texas, this time on a commercial air flight, I was seated next to an elderly man who had the most optimistic outlook I have ever seen. As we parted at the airport, he said something that really got my attention.

"Raymond," he said like he had known me all my life, "Make it a God filled day." The way he said it caught me by surprise.

"What did you say?" I turned and asked.

"Make it a God filled day" he repeated, and I could tell by his knowing smile that was exactly what he meant. Not have a good day, make it a God filled day. Even before he had disappeared into the crowd I had made up my mind that was exactly what I intended to do. Not just with that day, but with every day for the rest of my life.

Life is a precious thing, a gift of God, and when we are young, we think it will go on forever. So we drift through life thinking of all the things we'll do tomorrow. Understanding the temporariness of life is an essential part of making the most of our lives.

We all have choices how we will spend the seconds, the minutes, the hours and the days that make up the years of our lives. So we must choose wisely, taking advantage of the numerous opportunities to testify for Christ in our daily lives, to do right, to set a positive example, and to help others help themselves.

Looking for good, being good, and doing good. That's what being a Christian is all about. It doesn't mean abandoning our dreams, our desires for other successes, or missing out on any of the other joys and experiences that this wonderful life has to offer. It merely means being a Christian example in the eyes of our families, our friends, our business associates, our leaders and followers, and especially in the eyes of our Creator.

Christ had a choice how he would spend his life. Even facing death on the cross he still had a choice. Fortunately for us, He chose to give up his life to pay for our sins. Christ always made the right decision. By doing so He gave us a choice as to how we will spend our time here on Earth. He also gave us a choice as to how we well spend eternity. He only asks that we too make the right decisions and follow his example.

When I learned of the tumor, I was quite fortunate to already be a Christian. The threat to my life made me realize how much just being a Christian meant in my time of need. Because of Christ, even though I might be going to die, I didn't have to worry about where I would spend eternity. In spite of my short-comings, I had the promise of eternal life. That meant I could forget about the past, or the future, and focus my attention on being a Christian during my remaining days.

Through the grace of God, I survived. It was my Christian convictions that allowed me to conduct myself with courage and faith during those trying times, and for me and my family to survive the medical ordeal, the painful recovery, and the psychological trauma that followed over the coming months and years.

As I grow older, remember it's not the years, it's the miles, I am becoming more and more convinced that it doesn't matter whether one is an architect, a senator, a secretary, a homemaker, or whatever, each of us with God's help, can be a commander of our own destiny, if we choose to do so. But I am also keenly aware of the passing of time and the temporary nature of the life here on earth.

That tumor at the base of my brain made me acutely aware of the value of my limited time here on earth. And I have learned the lesson well.

Soon after we returned home from California following that second operation, a member of our church brought a special Christmas present to me. It was a small plaque, and on it were the words, "Today, is the first day of the rest of your life." It had, and still has great significance to me.

Since that time, each morning when I wake up, even before I get out of bed, I repeat my personal version of those beautiful words. "Today is the first day of the rest of my life." For what could be more precious than the God given promise of another day. There's so much to be done, so much to be learned, and so many wonderful things to share with those we love and know.

It's not a question of what to do, but what to do first. Over the years I come to fully realize that now, this moment, is the only time we can be sure of. And once it's gone, it's gone forever. So I keep on reminding myself that today, right now, is the most important day of the rest of my life. It's so easy to forget, even when you're one of the lucky ones like me who have seen the other side and had a second chance.

"Today is the day the Lord has made, let us rejoice and be glad in it," the *Bible* says.

There's another thing I do that keeps me aware of the value of time. Each night just before I go to bed, I ask myself the same question.

"Raymond," I say, "Have you really lived all you can today?" And usually, no matter how tired I am, I take the time to read another chapter, write another page, formulate another goal for the days to come, or spend a few more minutes in the company of the ones I love. Sometimes it is this extra effort at getting the most out of life that brings the greatest reward.

———————————

During my life since the operation I have enjoyed many hours of what I like to call "found time". One evening around the date of my son's twelfth birthday is especially vivid in my memory. He's grown now, and far from home making his own life, but the memories we built together will be ours to cherish forever. Like many kids his age at that time, he was very interested in space. The astronauts were his heroes. For his birthday we gave him a reflecting telescope; not a toy but a precision optical instrument.

The following Friday night, he and I spent several frustrating hours trying to locate M31, the giant Andromeda galaxy just east of the constellation Cassiopeia. I could find it in the binoculars, but never could get it to align in the telescope. Even in the telescope, I knew, it would have been but a faint blur, a cloudy mass of a billion stars, twice as large as our Milky Way, but two million light years away.

Finally, at about 9:30 p.m. we gave up. My eyes were blurring and my neck was aching from a day that had already seemed longer than usual. My son was obviously disappointed, but he thanked me for trying anyway. I think he could sense my feeling of defeat. We went in the house just in time to catch the last few minutes of *Falcon Crest*.

By the time the program ended, I was ready to go to bed. But first I wanted some fresh air. I went outside and looked up at the sky once more. Somehow the stars seemed brighter. I decided right then and there that I hadn't lived all I could that day.

"Bring the telescope Son" I yelled, "Let's try one more time."

Five minutes later I had the Andromeda galaxy in the field of view. It was spectacular, but under magnification, the movement of the earth, the passage of time was visibly evident. In a matter of seconds, I knew, the elusive galaxy would move out of the range of view. I was so excited, my hands were shaking. I didn't dare adjust the azimuth for fear of losing the treasure before my son had a chance to see it.

"Hurry Daddy," he said, "Move over, I want to see too."

He put his eye to the viewer, taking great care not to vibrate or move the telescope. His breath caught as he got his first glimpse of another galaxy. There was wonder in his eyes as he finally turned and looked up at me.

"It's there, Daddy, it's really there. And I can see it. Just like the astronauts."

Then he turned quickly back to the telescope. With hands steady as a surgeon's, he made the necessary adjustments needed to bring the galaxy back into the center of the field. For a long time he stared silently, speechless as the magnitude of what he was seeing sunk in.

For a while there, he was Galileo, Einstein, Werner Von Braun, and John Glenn all rolled into one. And yet he was a child alone, suddenly confronted by the unfathomable grandeur of creation, visibly conscious of the movement of the earth, and the perpetual passage of time as the beauty of the heavens moved across the field of view. Remembering the first time I saw a distant galaxy through my own telescope, I felt his joy.

"Here Daddy," he finally said, "You look while I go get the others. Before we tired of looking, every member of the family had seen a wonder few people see with their own eyes in a lifetime. Sure the image was dim, the viewing conditions poor, and our understanding of what we were seeing limited. But the wonder and sense of family communion at one with God's Universe was there. That alone made the extra effort worthwhile.

After the others went inside my son and I continued to marvel. "You know, Daddy," he said in his wisest voice, "it's hard to believe that one day I'll be up there, above all this distortion, and then I'll be able to see as far as I can dream."

Isn't that a wonderful thought? To be able to see as far as you can dream. And who knows? Maybe, just maybe, if it was God's Will, you could catch a glimpse of heaven.

Seven Times Seven

I wish that I might stop this day
To understand God's wondrous way
For once to feel with all my senses
Reality in its present tenses.

As an architect, I have always had a keen interest in ancient Greek history and philosophy. There's an interesting story from that period that clearly demonstrates how much one individual can influence the lives of others. Most people know something about the three great Greek philosophers, Socrates, Plato and Aristotle and their influence on the development of civilization as we know it today. Fewer people know that they directly interacted with one another.

Socrates came first. He was a walking teacher that traveled from place to place teaching lessons for a fee. His students were attracted by his great mind, unique ideas, tremendous personality and strength of character. It was Socrates who drank the hemlock, choosing to give up his life rather than his beliefs.

Plato was one of Socrates' students. It was Plato who wrote the Dialogues of Socrates, improving on his teacher's thoughts with his own to create many of the concepts that eventually became the basis for our government and democratic way of life.

Plato also had students. One of these was Aristotle. These three great minds followed in direct succession, each a teacher learning and improving on the concepts presented by the great mind that preceded him.

Aristotle had a historically famous student himself. For three years, beginning when Alexander was thirteen, Aristotle was private tutor to Alexander, the eleven-year-old son of King Phillip of Macedonia. The king commissioned Aristotle to teach his heir about math, politics, philosophy, and especially about how to influence people.

Legend has it that one day during a math class, Alexander is said to have asked his teacher an unusual question.

"How many," he asked in all seriousness, "is one?"

Today, the probable answers would be that one is a prime number; a single unit, being or thing; an absolute; or the first whole number above zero. Or maybe even, one half of two. But Aristotle had a better answer. He told Alexander to come back on the following day.

The next day, what he told the young man was a simple lesson in leadership that may possibly have changed the course of human history.

"In the areas of human affairs, of human influence," Aristotle told Alexander, "one can be a very great many indeed."

His young student, the future king of Macedonia, later became known as Alexander the Great, one of the greatest political leaders of all times, who extended Greek Civilization throughout the entire known world of that time.

My realization of the power of one, and how I might be a positive influence in the lives of others, came in a gradual and miraculously way.

Following the operation, it took several years to learn to cope with my physical disfigurement. Through necessity I managed to speak professionally about my work, but it was a number of years before I could bring myself to publicly live up to the promise I had made to God as I stood in the surf on that fateful day that changed my life. In fact, I subconsciously shut the commitment out, sufficiently at least, to allow me to ignore my obligation without feeling guilty. But something was incomplete in my new life in spite of my apparent business success and physical recovery, and I knew it.

My voice remained stilled but God's did not. On a particular Tuesday in the spring, at a weekly Rotary meeting, the option was no longer mine. As was tradition for new members it was my turn to stand up in front of the group and introduce myself officially. This noon meeting was larger than usual, for the Rotary Clubs of several area communities were meeting, not in our usual dining room, but in the atrium of the local Hilton, a very public place where people checking in and out or going to and from their rooms were constantly passing, outsiders often pausing to observe the meeting as they moved about their business.

Still self conscious about my disfigured face, there was a pit in my stomach as my turn to stand before the group rushed forward. My only comfort was that the audience was eating and talking even while the individuals at the podium were speaking, not necessarily being deliberately rude, but some at least visibly indifferent to the informal presentations being give. Most of the speaker's comments were autobiographical. "I was born in… I moved here in… I have two kids, one twelve and the other…. My wife's name… I work for… etc, etc."

Maybe the audience, not paying close attention, would fail to note my sagging face. Maybe I could get through this without calling too much attention to myself.

I hardly heard the scattered applause as my predecessor left the podium. A voice close by whispered in my ringing ear. "Raymond, its time." I looked around, searching for the source. Being deaf in one ear makes it difficult to tell the direction a voice has come from, especially when there are other voices or noises around. No one acknowledged my searching glance.

Nervously, heart pounding, I headed for the podium. "Tell them," the voice spoke again. "Not who you are, but what you know and believe. Remember the promise." This time I knew who it was.. God was speaking to me, calling in the promise. But more than that, he was there once more to help me face my demons. The fear vanished. A sense of well being, similar to what I felt on that fateful day I turned back to promise at the edge of the surf, filled my heart. The joy was back. Seven seconds later I was facing the crowd. A few looked up, but most just continued eating and their hushed conversations.

"My name is Raymond Burroughs," I said, amazingly clear considering my half-collapsed tongue and distorted mouth, "I'm an Architect, a dreamer and an eternal optimist. I'm also a Christian."

The room fell quiet, all eyes on me, waiting expectantly for me to continue. What seemed like an eternity passed before the words came again. This time it was not stage fright, self-consciousness, or fear which gave me pause, it was the realization that God was with me, forming the words I sensed would once again change my life. From that moment forward, I spoke clearly and without pause. The voice, I realized was mine, but the words were clearly a message from heaven.

"I've seen the miracle of God's healing grace", I continued, "And you too, as you see me standing here today, are seeing a miracle..." When my seven minutes were ended, there was no applause. No acknowledgement at all. Only silence as I returned to my table. I don't remember the rest of the program. The main speaker was up next, but I was listening to the music in my heart, trying to understand what had just happened. To this day I cannot tell you who the guest speaker was or what he was talking about.

I do remember the gentle comforting hands that reached out to touch me after the meeting was over. And the kind and comforting

words of those I passed as, still in a daze, I made my way across the
atrium on the way out of the building. As I reached the exit a friend
I had only recently met stepped in front of me. It was the pastor of
our church, relatively new to the community and someone's guest
on that day at Rotary. There were tears in his eyes.

"Raymond", he said, "that was the most touching testimonial I've heard in a long time."

"I'm not even sure what I said." I replied honestly.

"God knows," he said taking my hand. "Lay Sunday at the church
is next month. I'd like you to consider being our lay speaker."

Oh no, was my first thought. I had lived up to my end of
the bargain. Surely there was some mistake. It was one thing to
speak at Rotary to seventy people, another entirely to speak to
a whole congregation from the pulpit. Surely the man was kidding, caught up in the emotion of the moment.

"There will be two services", he continued. "I'd like you to
speak at both."

From somewhere out of my stunned silence, I heard myself
saying. "Well I guess so, if you think it's a good idea. How many
do you expect to attend?" I was learning real fast. I had free will,
but the will to resist God's plan wasn't something I really wanted
to do. No matter how hard it seemed I knew saying yes was the
right thing to do. If a little more was required to fulfill my side of
the deal, I would follow the path God opened up for me.

"Seven hundred," he said, "About Three hundred and fifty
fellow church members in each service"

My head was still spinning when I got back to the office.
Something had changed on that fateful day, but I wasn't sure
what. When I looked in the mirror the next morning, my face
didn't seem to look quiet as bad as it had the day before.

I have seldom felt as humble as I did that day when I stepped
into that pulpit. The words tumbled out in one long soliloquy of

hope, promise and fulfillment of God's promises. Not once did I stumble, not once did I stutter, but I was almost overcome by the promise of grace God led me to share. Tears dripped softly onto the unread scribbled notes I had intended to follow. In the front row, an elderly woman was weeping. A few rows back, several teenagers who had been whispering earlier, sat quietly, fully engaged in the message. A middle age couple further back leaned closer to each other, arms entwined, hanging on every word of hope. I thought of Pat, and what a blessing it had been to have her by my side all these years. It seemed the whole audience was holding its breath.

In a blink of an eye, it seemed, the first service was over. Not much later the second one was too, and somehow I was back in my chair behind the pulpit. I was exhausted, but my heart was soaring. Once more, God had seen me through. The promise was fulfilled. The debt paid. Now maybe I could get on with my ordinary life.

But God knew better. It wasn't meant to be. We were just beginning. The preacher invited me to stand with him in the foyer of the sanctuary as the congregation filed out. The response from the people was almost as overwhelming as the opportunity to speak had been. All expressed love. Many said they wanted to call on me later to tell me of an experience of their own. Some hugged my neck like a family I had never known.

One man held back until the crowd had thinned. I knew him as a friend, an outspoken Christian and a deacon in the largest Baptist church in the community.

"God works in strange ways", he said.

Whether he was alluding to seeing me in the pulpit or responding to my obvious surprise at seeing such a devout Baptist in a Methodist church at prime time on Sunday wasn't clear. I later learned he was there for the Christening of one of his grandchildren.

"I'd like you to speak to my Sunday school class week after next." The deacon wasn't known for beating around the bush.

This time I knew better than to delay. God was calling the shots on this gig. This and every one to come.

"Big class?" I asked.

"No, not so big. But the surveys say the television broadcast reaches about seven thousand."

I almost changed my mind. The camera never lies. For years, since my disfigurement I had avoided as many photographs as possible. And certainly no close-ups prior to an opportunity to close my mouth and turn the right cheek to the camera. But I knew the choice was not really mine.

"Just say when, and I'll be there." I blurted out with a crooked smile.

They taped the show, so I later got to see the program myself. In the interim, I recall, it dawned on me that the shape of my face wasn't what mattered to that audience at all. It was the message that really counted. And the promise of God for miracles in their own life.

As I was leaving the chapel where the class was held, another friend came up, a member of my own church. Why he was visiting a Baptist Sunday school class I never did find out. He headed a Christian Counseling service, well known for its positive impact on the youth of our area.

"Have you ever considered having your testimony published," he asked. Once more the seed was planted. God's plan continued to unfold. I hesitated for a few weeks, but before long I was at the computer, fleshing out the story and preserving it for all time. Writing it out wasn't easy, for to get to the good I had to relive the bad. Tears of sorrow and tears of joy mingled on the pages as I revised them before sending the manuscript off to a half dozen religious publications.

I had been published before. Two business books while in graduate school, a small article or two, and a few lines of poetry, so I wasn't surprised when the first rejection slips began to show up. Unlike the business publishers, the Christian responses were based on what they believed. Rejections true, but kind and courteous comments about the merit of my writing. "Keep on keeping on", one responded, "When it's God's will, your work will be published." Disappointed, I wasn't sure he was trying to convince himself or me.

The acceptance letter never came, but a phone call did. It was an editor from *The Presbyterian Journal.*

Yes, he would like to publish my story. He was truly touched and believed it would reach his readers. "Not a large publication," he said, "but we are doing great things for a magazine with a circulation of only seventy thousand.

I was overjoyed. This time I knew I had fulfilled my promise. Seventy thousand people represented a lot of souls, even if they all were already saved.

A few months after publication, I received a letter from the editor of *These Times Magazine.* The editor said he had seen my article in the Presbyterian Journal. With pride he told me his magazine reached homes all around the globe. "A readership of seven hundred thousand "he said.

God's plan was truly afoot now. A seven second decision, seventy Rotarians, seven hundred Methodist, seven thousand Baptist, seventy thousand Presbyterians, and now seven hundred thousand people around the world. It was a miracle. Another miracle that is. The realization of what was happening as a result of my responding to that desperate promise to God in those troubled times brought tears of joy to my eyes. Like the fishes in the miracle, God's blessing meant enough for everybody.

God's Purpose

Should I live a thousand years
Beyond the end of time
Would still, my Lord, not be enough
To share this joy of mine.

I've often wondered what my life would have been like without that resurrecting experience at the age of thirty-three. Of course I'll never know, at least not in this lifetime. Near the end of my short journey into eternity, my grandfather Papa told me I had to come back to this world. "God still has a purpose for you," he said.

So God sent me back. I've tried hard to figure it out, but to this day, I still don't know what that purpose is or whether I have accomplished any of it at all. What could it possibly be? Is it to witness to others, to care for my family, help those in need, create another architectural project, write this book, or what? I don't have a clue.

I truly believe God has a purpose for each of us in His universal plan for the eternal salvation of mankind. Toward that end, he has given each of us the unique gifts we need to do our part. Some of God's gifts are obvious. Our health, our intellect and our talents are clearly gifts of God. We cannot take credit for these gifts. But we can take credit for what we do with these gifts, and how we use the abundance resulting from them to help our families, our friends, and our fellow travelers in their search for meaning and salvation.

All of these gifts can play a significant part in fulfilling our role in God's plan. We need only discover what we do best, then, do that best, over and over again until we get it right. The key, I believe, is doing the right thing, the right way, for the right reasons. And then giving God the credit for our successes.

Each of our gifts is unique. In addition to giving me a second chance to fulfill my purpose, God has blessed me with the talent to be a good architect.

Since I opened my firm on that kitchen table three plus decades ago, I have had the opportunity to design many buildings and urban environments that have had a significant and positive impact on the quality of the lives of those who live, work, or play in the communities I serve. The work I have done touches almost every aspect of the lives of those who use these facilities, and spans a broad and diversified gamut of the quality built environments these people experience from cradle to grave. Some of my greatest earthly joys are hearing the laughter of children as they run through a play area or fountain I have designed, seeing the joyful tears of an elderly couple as they enjoy beautiful music in a near perfect acoustic environment, or listening to the stimulating conversations of students or workers who truly enjoy what they are doing, at least partly because of the pleasure and pride they find in being in a quality, state of the art facility.

A side benefit of my professional status is having the opportunity to touch the lives of others through what I say and do. Almost everybody has their fifteen minutes of fame. Mine have come, not because of me, but because of God giving me a second chance and the public nature of my work. If you do a public project, public interest, and in turn publication, are not far behind. In a small way, my projects have given me an open pulpit; a chance to speak out not only about my work, but also about what I have experienced and believe. I learned early in my career that as long as what I say adds value to the lives of those who read or hear, the opportunities will continue to come. It's what I call the "minor celebrity syndrome." Small audiences, but great opportunities to speak up for Christ.

For anyone who is interested, both the opportunities and benefits of witnessing for God are limitless. Consider public speaking. You know who gets the most benefit out of speaking up about the miracles of God in my life? Me! Before I started fulfilling my promise to God, I was self conscious about my image and terrified at the thought of speaking in a public forum. With God's help, and a self promise to always speak from the heart and give God credit for all I have or do, I soon came to love public speaking and found joy in turning a new thought, experience, or miracle into an opportunity to witness for Christ.

There have been speeches from pulpits and social podiums, articles in books and magazines; talks to graduating seniors; individual counseling of students headed for college; witnessing to individual clients, professional associates, employees, family and friends; motivational conversations to young and old alike; speeches at ribbon cuttings and building dedications; testimonies to prison inmates; giving comfort and hope to individuals seriously ill or approaching death; thousands of newspaper and handout articles, and now this book, all speaking of the power of God in my life.

Please understand, when I talk of my work, the buildings and places I have designed, the speeches I have made, the words I have written, and the counseling I have been privileged to give, I am not talking about me. I lost my ego when I lost my ability to smile. I'm talking about a continuing commitment, a never ending effort to fulfill God's purpose for me and the joy it has brought to my life.

It has not always been easy to convey that joy. As a part of that surgery when I was thirty-three years old, I lost the ability to smile. The tumor didn't end my life but it did threaten to take away many of the things in my life I had always taken for granted. Not only from me, but from those around me. For many years following that close encounter with the afterlife, my problem was no longer one of physical discomfort, at least not to a degree that affected my quality of life. Nor was it of psychological pain, at least not to a degree that justified self-pity or fear. But it was rather, one of social inconvenience to a degree that I felt apart and alone regardless of how others did or did not notice or react to my disfigurement. Without a smile, I always wondered whether my true moods and feelings were being communicated to those around me.

A smile is comforting not only to those around the one smiling, but also to the one doing the smiling. When I was a young man, my mother often reminded me to smile at an ugly girl and I would make her day. Not until I couldn't smile, or until I was the ugly one, did I realize just how much the little things we say and do can mean to those less fortunate or blessed than ourselves. It doesn't take wealth, power, or even much effort or time to do unto others as we would have them do unto us. In the end, it is often the one doing the good that benefits most from doing the right thing.

We are often judged, and we often judge, by outward appearances. Its human nature to question what is different about each other without taking time to understand what or why someone or something is different. Whether we call it bigotry, or prejudice, or simply ingrained distaste for the unfamiliar, in the end the result is the same. We are missing an opportunity to understand and support those who in all likelihood probably need our understanding and support the most. We are forgetting that we are all God's creation, the beloved children of God. We are forgetting that if someone is good enough for God, they ought to be good enough for us.

Just as we are different, we are also the same. We all have feel-ings, we all have dreams, and we all have the need for love and understanding. And we are all vulnerable to change.

That tumor was the worst, and the best, thing that ever hap-pened to me. It destroyed my life as I knew it at the time, but it made my life as I know it today. Before the surgery, I had spent most of my adult life trying to prove that I didn't need Christ or anyone else to accomplish my goals in life. I had chased dreams of wealth, success and superiority-missing many of the true values that make life worth living. My wife, my children, my family, my friends, my country, even my Christianity had taken a back seat so I could pursue what I wanted and what I believed to be of value to me. I was Raymond Burroughs, the great American hope, and anything I wanted was there for the taking.

And then it was all gone – the good looks, the confidence, the ability to sell anything to anyone, the dominance, the strength, and the clout and financial reserve built up over a dozen years of hard work and bluff. The Raymond Burroughs I knew died on that operating table and, through the Grace of God, a better man took his place.

The operations, that wonderful life after death experience and the physical and emotional roller coaster that followed were truly a turning point in my life. I reevaluated my life and the impact it had on others, and determined to live every day as if it were my last. I reordered my priorities and determined to respond to the goodness and help that the whole world had been holding out to me all along. I made a pact with God that from then on He would be Chairman of the Board, and that every decision I would make from that day forward would be after consultation with Him.

Since that time of life changing events and decisions, I have found witnessing to others in the name of Christ is not only a joy; it is a privilege, and an ongoing verification that God still has a purpose for my life. Unlike many people facing death, I got a second chance. Now it's up to me to decide what, when, where, and how much I will do to contribute to perpetuation of God's kingdom here on earth.

Every time I see a cross, I am reminded that we all have choices how we will spend the seconds, the minutes, the hours, and the days of our lives. In my case, it hasn't meant abandoning my career or my family responsibilities, or missing out on the many joys or experiences God's world has to offer. It merely means taking advantage of the numerous opportunities in my daily life to do God's will, to set a Christian example, and to tell others about the promise of immortality that can be found through Christ. In the end, that's where the true joy lies. Because of Christ, even in today's busy and often confusing world, we have a choice. Now and for eternity.

Beliefs
Summer 2008 / Lake Jackson, Texas

Deep within a yearning plea,
A mystic air of uncertain wants
Fill the heart with an ache of passion
Never still, never fulfilled, forever present
Begging eternally for consummate satisfaction.

Until we see the Light.

Life is an adventure, a beautiful though sometimes difficult journey of evolution. It is a complex continuum of time, events and association with others that combine as a whole to influence who we
are and what we believe at any given moment in our consciousness.

I don't know what you believe, but I know what I believe. I believe in God and the power of prayer. I believe in Christ, the Bible,
and God's promise of eternal life. I believe in the goodness of man,
and the harmony of the universe. I believe that all things work together for the good of those that love God. I also believe, and know,
there is a beautiful life after this one in a place called Heaven.

When I was a child I had a recurring dream about death. I
was at the bottom of an open grave. Looking up, I could see a
rectangle of blue sky silhouetting the heads of my parents and
family peering at me from far above. The view of their faces was
distorted by a steady flow of warm, silver raindrops cascading
down toward me. At some point in the dream I realized it wasn't
raindrops at all. It was the tears of those left behind. It seemed
strange that they would be crying and I would not. Not until

I had that brief glimpse of heaven did I understand what that dream was all about. It is not those who go to join Christ that suffer; it is those that are left behind.

The light I saw, I truly believe, was the heavenly radiance of God. As I traveled through time or space or wherever my spirit soared during that privileged odyssey, approaching closer and closer to the source of all that has or ever will be, there was no life review as others have witnessed, nor did I see an angel, Jesus, or God himself. There was only the Light and the promise of heaven to come.

Perhaps my journey ended too soon to experience those things. But I did see Papa who had died many years before. He was as real and alive and as loving as the grandfather who made me feel so special when I was a child. And there was a moment there at least, or perhaps an eternity, when all things seemed clear. There was literally nothing else I wanted or needed to know. The answers and questions were one and the same, and the peace of knowing and knowing I knew, for that time at least, was enough.

Over the past thirty or so years, since my short sojourn in the afterlife, I have had many occasions through words, example, deeds and my limited influence as an architect and a semi-public figure to try to live up to the promise I made to God on that lonely Gulf Coast beach a lifetime ago. I have tried with all my heart to keep the pact, making a conscious effort to share what I know and have experienced through the Grace of God with any that would listen. And yet I feel sure I have not said or done enough, that the most important opportunity to do God's will is the next one, and that only when I once again have the privilege to become one with the Light will I know whether I have finished the work I was sent back to do.

Until that time comes I will continue in my efforts to do more good than bad, strive to understand that which cannot be understood, and accept and love this gift of life for the miracle I know it to be.

In the end, I believe, it is not the years or the miles we travel that determine where we are in our perpetual search for salvation; nor is it the words we speak or the deeds we do; but it is rather, how we respond and accept through faith the gift of salvation God has given us through His Son Jesus Christ.

I have seen much pain, faced many challenges, and, in spite of it all, experienced more joy than any one man deserves. I am truly blessed.

God is good. God is great. And God smiles for me...

THE BEGINNING

Raymond can be contacted through the
GOD SMILES NETWORK.
www.godsmilesnetwork.org